THE PRESCHOOLER
&
THE LIBRARY

by
Ann D. Carlson

The Scarecrow Press, Inc.
Metuchen, N.J., & London
1991

British Library Cataloguing-in-Publication data available

Library of Congress Cataloging-in-Publication Data

Carlson, Ann D., 1952-
    The preschooler & the library / by Ann D. Carlson.
       p.   cm.
    Includes bibliographical references and index.
    ISBN 0-8108-2457-4 (alk. paper)
    1. Public libraries--Services to preschool children. 2. Pre-
school children--Books and reading. 3. Reading (Preschool)
I. Title. II. Title: Preschooler and the library.
Z718.1.C28   1991
025.5'277625--dc20   91-18073

For Ilyas and Zerrin

I sincerely believe that for the child, and the parent seeking to guide him, it is not half so important to know as to feel. If facts are the seeds that later produce knowledge and wisdom, then the emotions and the impressions of the senses are the fertile soil in which the seeds must grow. The years of early childhood are the time to prepare the soil. Once the emotions have been aroused—a sense of the beautiful, the excitement of the new and the unknown, a feeling of sympathy, pity, admiration or love—then we wish for knowledge about the object of our emotional response. Once found, it has lasting meaning. It is more important to pave the way for the child to want to know than to put him on a diet of facts he is not ready to assimilate.

—Rachel Carson, *The Sense of Wonder*, 1956

Contents

Preface

THIS is a book about preschoolers—children three and four years old—and libraries. Even though the major focus of the book is on service in public libraries, librarians or media specialists who work in schools with preschoolers should find much of what is said useful. Today many private schools and a growing number of public elementary schools have classrooms for three- and four-year-olds. In addition, there are quite a few preschools in high schools throughout this country that serve as early childhood education programs for the children of enrolled high school students and as training programs for those students who are interested in early childhood development.

Library service for preschoolers, although quite widespread today, is a relatively recent development in library history. It began after service for older children was firmly established and its spread paralleled the rise of the American picture book and the growth of the child study movement. Today library service for preschoolers is an important part of library work: a recent study conducted by the Department of Education reports that programs for children between three and five years of age make up over half of the total number of programs at the typical public library.[1] *The Preschooler & the Library* should help the

---

[1] Department of Education, National Center for Education Statistics, *Services and Resources for Children in Public Libraries, 1988–89* (Washington, D.C.: Government Printing Office, 1990), 25.

many librarians working with preschoolers and their parents, teachers and caregivers. It was written with them in mind.

The first two chapters present the historical background of library service to and schools for preschoolers. Chapter 1 provides a brief history of the rise of library service for preschoolers within the context of the development of library service for children in general. This includes service both for preschoolers and for parents and adults who work with them. Chapter 2 is an overview of the history of early childhood programs, such as nursery schools and child care centers.

The third chapter establishes a rationale for sharing books with preschoolers. Special emphasis is placed on the concept of emergent literacy, which has made librarians and other educators more aware of the role parents play when they introduce the riches of books and literature-centered activities to young children.

Chapter 4 describes how I developed the "schema," or outline, presented in Chapter 5. I consider Chapter 5 to be the heart of *The Preschooler & the Library*. It presents a compilation of salient developmental characteristics of three- and four-year-old children followed by implications for library programs drawn from these characteristics. I hope the schema will help eliminate some of the trial and error we resort to when searching for an appropriate match between the child and the library program. While reading this chapter, one should keep in mind that human development is continuous and only loosely synchronized with chronological age, and that library programs should ideally be based on children's developmental levels.

Chapter 6 discusses two special program considerations, multicultural education and preschoolers with special needs. Librarians may find the suggestions on how to select materials and how to plan and present programs helpful.

Chapter 7 examines the two types of literature-centered programs for preschoolers—programs presented by the librarian to preschoolers and programs offered to the parents, teachers, and caregivers of preschoolers. A checklist is offered at the end of the chapter that may be useful to librarians when they are planning, implementing, or evaluating a program. Central to this chapter (as it is throughout the book) is the belief that librarians must emphasize programs for parents and other adults if they are to instill a love for books and reading in children. Such programs are doubly effective because they meet the preschooler's need for repetition of books and enable us to reach a greater number of young children. Parents, teachers, and caregivers who spend time with children on a daily basis afford librarians great leverage in sharing books with young children.

The final chapter is an annotated selection of suggestions for further reading. It lists sources in child development, early childhood education, literary and literacy development, and library service and programs.

Acknowledgments

While writing this book, I benefited from time and knowledge many people generously contributed:

Mary Carlson drew the cover illustration.

Ates Dagli read the manuscript and produced the camera-ready copy.

Corinne Stich, Interlibrary Loan Coordinator at Rosary College, chased down many obscure and incomplete citations.

Zena Sutherland cast an experienced eye over the section on the rise of the American picture book in Chapter 1 and made valuable suggestions for the entire chapter.

Burton L. White graciously reviewed Chapters 4 and 5 and contributed some wise recommendations.

Patrick Williams applied his sharp mind to several chapters and offered much helpful criticism.

I thank them all.

Ann D. Carlson
Rosary College

A History of Library Service for Preschoolers

LIBRARY SERVICE for young children is a relatively recent development. It followed after library service for older children was firmly established and paralleled the rise of the American picture book along with the growth of the child study movement. This chapter is a brief history of the development of library service for preschoolers within the context of the development of service for children in general.

Libraries for Children: 1800 to 1876

Library work with children during the first half of the nineteenth century in the U.S. consisted of the sporadic efforts of kind-hearted men and women to provide children with books. The main purpose of these first libraries was to provide didactic materials for children.

An often cited example of an early effort is that of the library of West Cambridge, Massachusetts, which was begun in 1835 with a bequest from Ebenezer Learned, the town's physician. In a 1913 article, Alice Jordan, a pioneer in children's work, described the librarian as "Uncle" Dexter, who made hats during the week and opened the library to children on Saturdays.[1] Dr.

---

[1] It should be noted that Dexter was not the only one working during the week in West Cambridge (now Arlington), a textile mill town. In 1832 about 40% of all factory workers in New England were

Learned insisted that the books be chosen by the selectmen, ministers of the Gospel, and the town's physicians.[2] In other small libraries (such as those in Salisbury, Connecticut; Dublin, New Hampshire; Allegheny, Pennsylvania; and Peterborough, New Hampshire) there were individual initiatives to put books in the hands of children in the early decades of the nineteenth century. These were isolated instances which should not be considered as the foundation for later library service to children.

The Rise of Children's Library Work: 1876 to 1900

The year 1876 is a landmark date in public library history. During the country's centennial celebrations, a group of librarians met in Philadelphia and formed the American Library Association (ALA). *Library Journal*, whose purpose was to record the history and progress of the public library movement, was also launched. Finally, a national report, *Public Libraries in the United States of America*, was issued by the U.S. Department of Education.

There was no mention of children's service per se in the 1876 report, but William I. Fletcher, a public librarian from Hartford, Connecticut, who would later become president of the ALA, contributed an essay titled "Public Libraries and the Young." Elizabeth Nesbitt, a library educator, maintains that this essay "well may be taken as marking the turning point in the conception of the public library as something more than a storehouse of culture, with the ultimate inevitable change of attitude toward the right of children to have access to a public library."[3] In his essay, Fletcher questioned the public library's responsibility to the young regarding two issues: the need of "cultivating a taste for good reading" and age restrictions.

---

between the ages of 7 and 16, and the development of the textile industry depended heavily on child labor.

[2]Alice M. Jordan, "A Chapter in Children's Libraries," *Library Journal* 38 (January 1, 1913): 20–21.

[3]Elizabeth Nesbitt, "Library Service to Children," *Library Trends* 3 (October 1954): 118.

The question of whether tawdry fiction should be found in the public library for adults[4] or children[5] was hotly debated. Sensationalism was the culprit, produced in large measure in children's books by William T. Adams, who wrote over one hundred adventure series books under the pseudonym Oliver Optic, and by Horatio Alger. While this debate did not directly concern young children, it resulted in book selection aids. These tools included books for preschoolers and became buying guides for libraries. One of the earliest, *Books for the Young: A Guide for Parents and Children*, which was compiled by Caroline M. Hewins, librarian of the Hartford Public Library, was published in 1882. That Hewins's list ran through several editions may be viewed as evidence of the growth in publishing of books for young children and their acceptance by librarians. Three editions of her list are discussed in the next section.

Addressing the issue of age limitations, William Fletcher claimed there was "no usage on this point which can be called common, but most libraries fix a certain age, as twelve or fourteen, below which candidates for admission are ineligible." There were even libraries that hung signs that read "Children and dogs not admitted."[6]

Fletcher recommended that age restrictions be abandoned. A nonrestrictive policy was the "right solution ... and most consistent with the idea of the public library." He reasoned that the cultivation of good taste in books "cannot be begun too early," arguing that:

No after efforts can accomplish what is done with ease early in life in the way of forming habits either mental or

---

[4]Patrick Williams discusses this in "The Fiction Problem, 1876–1896," in *The American Public Library and the Problem of Purpose* (Westport, Conn.: Greenwood Press, 1988).

[5]Richard Darling has chronicled this debate in *The Rise of Children's Book Reviewing in America, 1865–1881* (New York: Bowker, 1968).

[6]Robert Ellis Lee, *Continuing Education for Adults through the American Public Library, 1883–1964* (Chicago: American Library Association, 1966), 33.

moral, and if there is any truth in the idea that the public library is not merely a storehouse for the supply of the wants of the reading public, but also and especially an educational institution which shall create wants where they do not exist, then the library ought to bring its influences to bear on the young as early as possible.[7]

Through the 1880s and early 1890s, "children" in library parlance continued to denote those over the age of twelve. Fletcher's essay continued to provoke discussion about the age limitations on library use as well as on the quality of books published for children throughout the profession.[8] At the 1894 ALA conference held at Lake Placid, Lutie Stearns's "Report on Reading for the Young" summarized questionnaire replies from 145 libraries concerning the advisability of abolishing the age limit for children, limitations on books issued to children and teachers, special rooms for children, and the desirability of having a special attendant to serve children. Less than a third of the responding libraries had no age limits while seventy percent reported that the age limit varied between eight and sixteen years, with the average age requirement being thirteen. Comments on this query included: "Our books are not suited to young people," "We must draw the line somewhere," and "We have an age limit of twelve years for no other reason than because we are the victims of an absurd library custom, adopted before we knew better." Others, such as John Cotton Dana, then of the Denver Public Library, responded: "We give a child a card as soon as he can read. Children too young to read get cards for books to be read to them."

Lutie Stearns, head of circulation at the Milwaukee Public Library, put forward her strong views on the issue of age

---

[7]William I. Fletcher, "Public Libraries and the Young," in U.S. Bureau of Education, *Public Libraries in the United States of America: Their History, Condition and Management: Part 1* (Washington, D.C.: U.S. Government Printing Office, 1876), 414.

[8]Alice Hazeltine's *Library Work with Children* (New York: H.W. Wilson, 1917) is a collection of papers and addresses that chronicle the removal of the age barrier.

restrictions as follows: "We deprecate the spirit which prompts a librarian to say, 'We prefer to transact business with older persons as we lose time in making infants understand.' Opposed to this are the words of another who writes, 'Each assistant has instruction by no means to neglect the children for the adults.'"[9]

The view put forth by Fletcher and persistently supported by librarians such as Lutie Stearns slowly but steadily became reality. Libraries began according children entry and in some cases borrowing privileges. As libraries abolished age limits, however, the children poured in and created the need for a new type of service. For example, Caroline Hewins mentions one community where, according to the local paper, eighty-one children visited the adult reading room of the library on February 25, 1900, all quiet and orderly. The accompanying photograph of the reading room with one man, one woman, and fifty-one children in it finally caused the city to provide a separate room for children.[10]

Between 1890 and 1900 children's rooms opened in libraries throughout the country. Many libraries claim the distinction of being the first to establish separate children's departments, which indicates that the idea had reached the point where it was put into practice in many places virtually simultaneously. Based on a survey conducted in 1897, Mary Wright Plummer, Director of the Pratt Institute Free Library and Library School, reported that there were children's rooms in thirteen cities with plans for more in several others. She emphasized the need for adequate children's book collections and a high quality of service to children. Plummer pleaded that serious consideration of pro- fessional children's librarians was now needed.[11] She led the

---

[9]Lutie E. Stearns, "Report on Reading for the Young," *Library Journal* 19 (December 1894): 81–87.

[10]Caroline M. Hewins, "How Library Work with Children Has Grown in Hartford and Connecticut," *Library Journal* 39 (February 1914): 91–99.

[11]Mary Wright Plummer, "The Work for Children in Free Libraries," *Library Journal* 22 (November 1897): 679–86.

way in 1895 by selecting Anne Carroll Moore, who had just completed her training in children's librarianship at Pratt Institute Library School, to administer the children's room at the Pratt Institute Free Library.

By the end of the century the pioneers, such as Caroline Hewins whose annual reports to the ALA kept service to children a pressing issue and Lutie Stearns whose 1894 report marked a general acceptance by the profession of children's service in libraries, had sown the seeds which would produce one of the most exciting periods in children's librarianship.

An Examination of Caroline Hewins's Lists: 1897 to 1915

Caroline Hewins, librarian of the Hartford Public Library, grew up in an environment well furnished with books and good literature. She wanted children to know the pleasures to be gotten from Walter Crane's and Randolph Caldecott's illustrations and Howard Pyle's and Andersen's tales. Hewins knew, however, that these books were competing with the cheap fictional works of the then popular "Four Immortals," as she called Oliver Optic, Martha Finley, Horatio Alger, and Harry Castleman. One of the ways she hoped to stimulate better reading by children was to prepare annotated lists of good books for children.[12]

A comparison of three editions of Hewins's *Books for Boys and Girls*,[13] published for the ALA Publishing Section by the Library Bureau, reflects the growth in the number of books available for preschoolers.[14] During the eighteen-year interval

---

[12]A biography of Hewins is provided by Mary E.S. Root in *Pioneering Leaders in Librarianship* ed. Emily Miller Danton (Chicago: American Library Association, 1953).

[13]Caroline M. Hewins, *Books for Boys and Girls: A Selected List* (Boston: Press of Rockwell and Churchill for the American Library Association, 1897); 2nd ed. (Boston: ALA Publishing Board, 1904); and, 3rd ed. (Chicago: American Library Association, 1915).

[14]Hewins's *Books for the Young: A Guide for Parents and Children*, published in 1882, was already a "collector's rarity" in 1943 according to

between the first and the third editions, there is significant growth in the initially meager selection of books for older children and moderate growth in the selection of books for younger children.

The first edition compiled by Hewins was published in 1897 and contained 31 pages. In the introduction of this literally small (it was 13 cm by 8 cm) book she states that the list is intended to help the smaller public library and fathers, mothers, and teachers in buying books. Hewins's "Illustrated Books for the Youngest Children" section lists only eleven titles by three of the major English illustrators of the day, Randolph Caldecott, Walter Crane, and Kate Greenaway, plus *Mother Goose's Melodies* published by Houghton. As an aside, it is interesting to note that Hewins decided not to include "stories of the present day in which children die, are cruelly treated, or offer advice to their fathers and mothers, and take charge of the finances and love affairs of their elders" since such books were not good reading for children in happy homes. In addition, Hewins reasoned that less fortunate children preferred and should be encouraged to read "fairy-tales or histories rather than stories of life like their own."

The second edition of 56 pages published in 1904 grew not only in size (20 cm by 12 cm) but also in the number of titles. The "Illustrated Books for the Youngest Children" section contained 23 titles. The eleven titles by Caldecott, Crane, and Greenaway were carried over from the previous edition, the Mother Goose title was omitted, and 12 new titles appeared by eight other authors. These included Helen Bannerman's *Story of Little Black Mingo*, *Story of Little Black Quibba*, and *Story of Little Black Sambo*. In the preface Hewins says that no one can ever have the resources and the joy that books bring "who has not had them from earliest childhood." Hewins and other librarians

---

Effie L. Power's *Work with Children in Public Libraries* (Chicago: American Library Association, 1943, p. 17), and I was not able to locate a copy for the comparison. *Books for Boys and Girls* is in the same style as that of the 1882 list.

like her would have undoubtedly welcomed more than the 23 books on the list, some of which were inappropriate for the small child even then, such as Heinrich Hoffman's *Slovenly Peter*.

The third and last edition was 112 pages long and was published in 1915. It was clear that the field of children's publishing had experienced a significant growth between the last two editions. Whereas the 1904 edition did not have a table of contents, the last edition contained one with 45 separate sections, such as "Fifty Must-Haves," which was a list Hewins suggested for home buying, "Fairy Tale and Wonder Stories," "Dolls," "Stories of Home, School, Etc.," "Indians and Ranch Life," and "Voyages, Shipwrecks and Desert Islands." The 1915 edition included a new section, "A Few Foreign Picture-Books," in addition to the "Illustrated Books for the Youngest Children" section continued from the previous editions.

Forty titles were included in the "Illustrated Books" section. The Bannerman books of the 1904 edition were deleted and titles by Leslie Brooke, E. Boyd Smith, and Peter Newell appeared. It is interesting to see that six different Mother Goose editions are listed, including those illustrated by Blanche Fisher Wright, Jessie Willcox Smith, and Arthur Rackham. Curious omissions are books by Beatrix Potter, including *The Tale of Peter Rabbit* which had been published in 1901. The fifteen titles in "A Few Foreign Picture-Books" were published by Brentano and written by eight authors, including Elsa Beskow and Carl Larsson.

A growing market for children's books emerged during the eighteen years spanned by these lists. Before the turn of the century, publishers were not willing to invest in children's books. Publisher Frederic Melcher claimed: "The great difficulty in publishing children's books in 1898 was the restricted size of the market. The public library requirements were not large ... and the public schools ... were confining their book interests to text-books. The best bookstores had a highly intelligent public of limited scope."[15] During the following few years, however, many small book shops and large department stores slowly began stocking children's books. Libraries also began buying children's books and librarians helped booksellers by distributing lists, such as Hewins's, to children and their parents.

Advancement of Children's Library Work: 1900 to 1920

The first two decades of the century were a whirlwind time for children's library service. Andrew Carnegie stimulated its growth through his philanthropic contribution of funds for public library buildings which had designated space for children's books. State and federal legislation curbing child labor and mandating school attendance provided leisure for many children who had previously spent ten hours a day in factories. The influx of immigrants, often with large families, into major cities throughout the country also had an effect since the native-born saw the library as a vehicle for assimilating the new citizens into American life.

These twenty years were a time of experimentation in children's librarianship. It was also during this time that the employment of professionally trained children's librarians began. They had first formed the Section for Children's Librarians of the American Library Association during the Montreal Conference in 1900. This period also marked the beginning of the influence that children's librarians would have on children's bookmaking and publishing,[16] a field that rapidly grew.

Most libraries established services that dealt directly with the child. An important exception was the Newark Public Library, which employed a different technique. An English librarian and researcher, Gwendolen Rees, wrote that "such

[15]Frederic G. Melcher, "Thirty Years of Children's Books," in *Children's Library Yearbook: Number 1* (Chicago: American Library Association, 1929), 5.

[16]Sara Fenwick, "Library Service to Children and Young People," *Library Trends* 25 (July 1976): 329–60.

activities as story hours, reading clubs, home libraries and
provision for young children are relegated to the background, on
the principle that personal contact with the children is only
possible in the case of a very small proportion of them, and that
it is more satisfactory to reach them through the teachers."[17]
John Cotton Dana, librarian of the Newark Public Library,
defended this type of service because he viewed the city school
system with its infinitely greater resources and teachers as better
equipped to promote children's reading than librarians who
were "usually less well equipped in the pedagogic art." He
believed that the key lay at the "teacher's door":

> As she outnumbers ... assistants in libraries a hundred
> times; as she comes in personal contact with her pupils
> about a thousand hours in a year against ten to twenty
> for the librarian; as experience shows that she can guide
> the reading and book-using habits of her pupils if and as
> she will, then the children's work in the library should
> be, chiefly, not with children, but for children; not in
> guiding children, but in guiding teachers.[18]

During the first part of the century, leaders such as Anne Carroll
Moore of the New York Public Library, Clara Whitehill Hunt of
the Brooklyn Public Library, Frances Jenkins Olcott of the
Carnegie Library in Pittsburgh, Alice Jordan of the Boston Public
Library, and Caroline Burnite (Walker) and Effie Lee Power of
the Cleveland Public Library set high standards for themselves
and their profession. These women zealously promoted library
service to children. Still, little attention was given to the child
who was not yet in school. This was in part due to the fact that
there were relatively few books for the young child. Instead, the
focus was on the reading child who needed guidance to the
many good books that were available.

---

[17]Gwendolen Rees, *Libraries for Children* (London: Grafton, 1924),
103–4.

[18]John Cotton Dana, "The Legitimate Field of the Municipal Public
Library: Work for and with Children," *Library Association Record* 16
(November 14, 1914): 472.

Concern for Content in Children's Books: 1915 to 1925

With the establishment and expansion of library service for children underway, librarians and publishers were focusing on children's reading. The years from 1915 to 1925 were very exciting and at the same time very turbulent. A handful of major figures appeared who "stood at the crossroads and led the way into the promised land of children's books, encouraging struggling artists and authors, studying new techniques of printing and illustrating, ferreting out the needs of boys and girls for this book and that as the years passed."[19]

At the beginning of this period, May Massey was the editor of *Booklist*, but she left in 1923 to become head of the children's book department of Doubleday and later went to Viking. Louise Seaman Bechtel had had the corresponding position at Macmillan Company since 1919, and Virginia Kirkus became the first children's books editor at Harper and Brothers. In 1924 Bertha Mahony Miller launched *The Horn Book Magazine*, which was to have a major influence on the literary quality of children's books.[20] That same year, Anne Carroll Moore, Supervisor of Work with Children at the New York Public Library, began writing her famous *Three Owls* (author, artist, and critic) weekly page for the *New York Herald Tribune*, in which she argued the need for high standards for authors, illustrators, and publishers.

Meanwhile, as the child study movement and early childhood education movement grew in this country, it became evident, especially to nursery school teachers, that there was a

---

[19]Dora V. Smith, "Children's Books—Yesterday and Today," *ALA Bulletin* 51 (April 1957): 256.

[20]*The Horn Book Magazine* was published by the Boston Bookshop for Boys and Girls which had been established by the Women's Educational Union. In its first issue, its purpose was stated: "We blow our horns for the best in Children's Literature, for books beautifully written and finely illustrated.... Our jovial huntsmen shall lead children over the hills and far away to the magic land of storybooks, where twentieth century boys and girls may follow and adventure." (October 1924, p.30)

dearth of realistic stories for the young child. This was true for older children as well. In an article including a list of recommended books for children from two to ten years of age that appeared in *The Bookman* in 1920, only two of the titles were realistic stories: Bergengren's *Jane, Joseph, and John* (1918) and E. Boyd Smith's *Chicken World* (1910).[21]

Many teachers, especially those of young children, argued that the events of the First World War showed that children needed factual materials, not fairy tales, if they were to be able to face the changing world ahead. Theorists of the child study movement claimed that young children were curious about experiences in their own surroundings. John Dewey and his followers who began the Progressive Education movement maintained that a child learned through solving real-life problems. Educators argued that the content of stories should reflect "a study of child life": Animals and people should be realistically presented rather than fantasized, and seeds should grow into proper plants with care, rather than through the use of magic wands.

Lucy Sprague Mitchell, a follower of Dewey and a nursery school teacher at Bank Street School in New York City, published *The Here and Now Story Book* in 1921.[22] After Mitchell took her classes out for walks in Greenwich Village, they talked about the river, the stores, the horses, or whatever else they had seen. Mitchell wrote these stories down and they became the content of her books. The stories emphasized the way things feel, sound, smell, and look to the small child, and had little or no plot. In a later edition, she claimed that "the attempt to amuse children by presenting them with the strange, the bizarre, the unreal, is the unhappy result of adult blindness. Children do

---

[21]Anne Carroll Moore, "Children under Ten and Their Books," *The Bookman* 50 (1919–20): 640–42.

[22]Lucy Sprague Mitchell, *The Here and Now Storybook* (New York: Dutton, 1921).

not find the unusual piquant until they are firmly acquainted with the usual."[23]

A turbulent debate continued over whether imaginative literature was appropriate for young children. The fortunate upshot was that the discussion focused attention on the need for more books for the young child, realistic or not. Evidence from the next decade indicates that publishers were paying attention.

New offset printing processes brought from Europe after the War made this need easier to meet. Multiple printing and reproduction techniques made it possible to manufacture beautifully illustrated books at a reasonable cost. Prior to this technique, illustrations had to be tipped into the books on separate sheets; now, they could become an integral part of the story. The war also brought to the United States the first of a stream of talented artists such as Miska Petersham, Fritz Eichenberg, Ludwig Bemelmans, and Feodor Rojankovsky, who would help to develop the picture book for young children.

The Rise of the American Picture Book: The 1930s

A number of talented artist-illustrators contributed to the rise of the picture book for young children. In 1928 Wanda Ga'g, who was born in Minnesota in an environment rich in old-world folklore, wrote and illustrated *Millions of Cats*, which, according to Zena Sutherland, ushered in what came to be known as "The Golden Thirties" of picture books.[24] Writing about the book, Ruth Hill Viguers said:

It has all the sureness of the tale told for generations. At a time when originality of artistic expression was only beginning to be encouraged, Wanda Ga'g dared to be herself, and the immediate success of her first book proved that children were ready for such daring

[23]Lucy Sprague Mitchell, *Here and Now Story Book*, rev. and enlarged ed. (New York: Dutton, 1948), 16.

[24]Zena Sutherland, *Children and Books* 7th ed. (Glenview, Ill.: Scott, Foresman, 1986), 143.

expression which was at the same time so perfectly
compatible with the storytelling tradition. The pictures
of *Millions of Cats* tell the story with vitality and atmosphere; yet the story can stand alone.[25]

This book indeed heralded The Golden Era. The 1930s saw the
publication of picture books for young children expand from a
handful of titles a year to an annual parade, an oddity when
one considers that the U.S. was entering the Great Depression.
Artists who had been experimenting through the twenties saw
their books come to life, in part because the photo-offset litho-
graphic technique made possible large numbers of illustrated
books at reasonable cost. Originality was the keynote of this
decade's picture books.

Marjorie Flack wrote and illustrated two classics of action,
simplicity, and realism, *Angus and the Ducks* in 1930 and *Angus
and the Cat* in 1931. Flack's books are of the "here and now"
style. Angus, a little black Scottie, was a believable dog who
neither spoke nor did anything a real dog would not do, but he
was as curious as the children he entertained.

That same year, Mary Steichen Martin and the well-known
photographer Edward Steichen produced *The First Picture Book*
(1930), a unique book in that it was composed entirely of full-
page black and white photographs of real objects found in the
everyday life of a small child. *The Second Picture Book* (1931)
contained a little more advanced photographs, but it was also
intended for the nursery-school-aged child. Lena Towsley's
Peggy and Peter (1931) with its full-page photographs showing
what a young boy and girl do during the day from waking up to
going to sleep, and a sequel *Sally and Her Friends* (1932) were
similar in format. Unlike the Martin and Steichen books, these
included a sentence or a part of a sentence on the page opposite
each photo telling the story. It is unfortunate that these "camera
books," as they were called, with their exquisite photographs,

[25]Cornelia Meigs et al., *A Critical History of Children's Literature*
(New York: Macmillan, 1953), 583.

are seldom found on lists of significant books in children's literature texts. They were widely used and very popular in spite of their two-dollar price.[26]

The first part of the decade included several other noteworthy picture books for preschoolers: Maud and Miska Petersham's *Christ Child* (1931), Marjorie Flack's *Ask Mr. Bear* (1932), and Lois Lenski's *Little Family* (1932) and *Little Auto* (1934). In the later part of the decade, Munro Leaf's *The Story of Ferdinand* (1936) illustrated by Robert Lawson delighted young children as well as their parents. *Mittens* by Clare Newberry, which was published in 1936, signaled the first of several popular picture books she would create about kittens. That same year, the fine English artist Edward Ardizzone created Tim who, in *Little Tim and the Brave Sea Captain*, would have sea adventures that were within the realm of what young children could imagine.

In 1937, Theodor Geisel, writing under the pen name Dr. Seuss (his middle name), produced *And to Think That I Saw It on Mulberry Street*, an extravagantly nonsensical, rhymed narrative with zany, bright-color drawings that delighted young children. *Andy and the Lion* by the sculptor and artist James Daugherty, with its powerful black and white illustrations, was produced the same year (1938) that Claire H. Bishop's *The Five Chinese Brothers* appeared. The decade ended with the publication of four classics in 1939: Margaret Wise Brown's *The Noisy Book*,[27]

---

[26]Committee on Library Work with Children of the American Library Association under the Chairmanship of Mary S. Wilkinson, and the Research Department of the Winnetka Public Schools under the Supervision of Vivian Weedon and Carleton Washburne, *The Right Book for the Right Child: A Graded Buying List of Children's Books* (New York: John Day, 1933) has a preschool list of books for two- to five-year-olds prepared by Rose Alschuler and other teachers of the Winnetka nursery school and kindergarten. Over fifty titles are given, including the "camera books" mentioned above, Mitchell's *Here and Now Story Book*, and the Ga'g and Flack books.

[27]Brown, who wrote under the pseudonyms of Golden MacDonald, Juniper Sage, and Timothy Hay, was a student in Lucy Sprague Mitchell's experimental writing group and contributed to Mitchell's

Ludwig Bemelmans's *Madeline*, Hardie Gramatky's *Little Toot*, and Virginia Lee Burton's *Mike Mulligan and His Steam Shovel*.

By the end of the decade, the picture book was firmly established. Events such as the research to determine children's preferences in picture book illustration,[28] the *Bibliography of Books for Young Children* launched by the Association for Childhood Education International in 1937, and the endowment of the Caldecott Medal by Frederic Melcher in 1938 for the best picture book of the year[29] demonstrate this without a question.

Development of Library Service for Preschoolers

Sara Fenwick contends that if the first two decades of the century can be described as a time of innovation and enthusiasm in children's service, then the following decades are best termed as those of standardization and broadening horizons.[30] In the mid-1930s, a few children's librarians, believing that service for preschoolers was a way of broadening library service, initiated a story hour for children who were not yet in school and called it the preschool story hour. Such librarians were challenging the popularly-held notion that a "children's library room is intended primarily for use by boys and girls between the ages of six and fifteen."[31]

Four developments contributed to the expansion of service for preschoolers. First of all, a sizable selection of good picture books was becoming available. The picture book was, as the

---

second *Here and Now Story Book* (1937). Louise Seaman Bechtel's touching essay about "Brownie" (Brown) is found in *Books in Search of Children* (New York: Macmillan, 1969).

[28]"Children's Preferences in Book Illustrations, conducted by the Association for Art in Childhood," *Publishers' Weekly* 126 (December 30, 1939): 2321.

[29]Cornelia Meigs et al., *A Critical History of Children's Literature* (New York: Macmillan, 1953), 431.

[30]Sara I. Fenwick, "Library Service to Children and Young People," *Library Trends* 25 (July 1976): 329–60.

[31]Effie L. Power, *Library Service for Children* (Chicago: American Library Association, 1930), 123.

librarian of the Los Angeles Public Library described it, "a vehicle upon which the children's librarian can take her group of children far way into the lands of fun and fantasy."[32] Creative librarians wanted to find a way of introducing preschoolers to the beautifully illustrated and written books. The preschool story hour seemed to be "the natural medium through which the introduction may be made."[33] The contents of a typical story hour included picture books, songs and chants, musical activities, simple poems and finger plays, simple dramatics and stretching activities, and flannel board stories. (More recently, films, filmstrips, and videos have been added.)

Secondly, parents began to demand story hours for their small children. Handbooks written before the 1930s cautioned librarians against allowing "restless preschoolers" to attend story hour since they would "spoil the effect which the story hour ought to have on the older children."[34] Nonetheless, parents kept bringing their preschoolers to story hours regardless of age restrictions, to the dismay of some librarians. Articles by librarians writing about why they started preschool story hours stated a common refrain: "The preschoolers were ruining our school-age story hours. We became aware that there was a definite need in the community." In some instances, parents not only initiated the library programs but conducted them.[35]

Thirdly, the increasing number of school libraries being established by city school systems was having its effect on the public library's service to children. National standards written by committees of the ALA and the National Education Association (NEA) were in place for high school libraries by 1918 and for elementary school libraries by 1925. Leaders in the school

[32]Florence Sanborn, "How to Use Picture-Story Books," *Library Journal* 74 (February 15, 1949): 272.

[33]Ethel C. Karrick, "Pre-School Story Hour," *ALA Bulletin* 41 (November 1947): 445.

[34]Clara Whitehill Hunt, *Library Work with Children* (Chicago: American Library Association, 1924), 22.

[35]Flora E. Hottes, "New Horizons for the Library," *ALA Bulletin* 35 (May 1941): 326.

movement, such as Lucile Fargo, who wrote *The Library in the School* and *The Program for Elementary School Library Service*[36] in 1930, were beginning to have a far-reaching influence. Some children had ready access to their school libraries and no longer needed some of the services offered by their public libraries. Preschoolers could comfortably fill the gap that school-age children left.

Finally, the fourth and most important development was the growth of the child study movement which called attention to the importance of the preschool period of development. Books, such as Alice Dalgliesh's *First Experiences with Literature*,[37] alerted parents, teachers, and librarians to the need for introducing books to small children. As one librarian said, "We are of the firm opinion that by opening the doors of the public library to the child when he is at the picture-book age, we are establishing a solid foundation for a better education and a higher quality of literacy."[38] Another librarian pointed to the preschool story hour as one way of laying the necessary foundation:

> Little minds need to be fed the correct diet the same as little bodies. They are full of curiosity and are reaching out for information. Stories and books will fill a great need here, and if children are to love good books and reading later in life we must nourish minds properly at this early age.... The library preschool story hour is an educational program for all which will bear fruit now and later.[39]

---

[36]Lucile F. Fargo, *The Library in the School* (Chicago: American Library Association, 1930) and *The Program For Elementary School Library Service* (Chicago: American Library Association, 1930).

[37]Alice Dalgliesh, *First Experiences with Literature* (New York: Scribner, 1932).

[38]Helen E. Waite, "Library Adventures for the Youngest," *Wilson Library Bulletin* 19 (January 1945): 328.

[39]Candace McDowell Chamberlin, "The Preschool Story Hour," *Library Journal* 69 (November 1, 1944): 928.

In library literature the Detroit Public Library is often cited as the first to offer preschool story hours beginning in 1935.[40] As in the case of the first library to establish a separate children's department, other libraries claim the distinction,[41] which indicates that many librarians had independently embraced the same idea.

By the mid-1940s, preschoolers were securing a place in the American public library. An increasing number of articles about preschool service, especially about preschool story hours, appeared in the literature. Textbooks used for training children's librarians, such as Effie Lee Power's widely-used handbook, began to mention preschool service:

> The first pleasurable book experiences of little children are enjoyment of pictures and recognition of familiar stories in text. With these two points in mind, the children's librarian puts books into their hands with brief comments, reads informally to small groups gathered around a library table, talks with individual children about the books they bring to her attention, and tells them stories. She holds story hours at which storytelling picture books are shown and read aloud. These have proved very popular, so much so that mothers have been persuaded to attend and bring children of preschool age. These picture book hours encourage similar enjoyment of books in the home. Fathers can be persuaded that reading aloud from a well selected picture book before the children's supper hour gives them a happy contact with their little children.[42]

---

[40]Elizabeth H. Gross, *Public Library Service to Children* (Dobbs Ferry, N.Y.: Oceana, 1967), 96.

[41]In research conducted in 1982 for my doctoral dissertation, I queried librarians about when their libraries began programs for children under the age of three. One librarian responded that two-year-olds were a part of the library's preschool story hours begun in 1921. This is earlier than any claims in the literature. Since all questionnaires were returned anonymously, I do not know the name of the library.

[42]Effie L. Power, *Work with Children in Public Libraries* (Chicago: American Library Association, 1943), 88.

Meanwhile, the 1940s were also a time when children's book publishing continued in spite of wartime shortages of paper and cloth and the rationing of metal for printing plates. It was a decade that felt the influence of the children's book editors of the thirties along with some new powerful ones such as Ursula Nordstrom at Harper & Row, Margaret K. McElderry at Harcourt Brace, and Elizabeth Riley at Thomas Y. Crowell. Picture books of the decade are remarkable for their variety of form and theme. Some like Hans A. Rey's *Curious George* (1941), Robert McCloskey's *Make Way for Ducklings* (1941), Virginia Lee Burton's *The Little House* (1942), Margaret Wise Brown and Clement Hurd's *The Runaway Bunny* (1942) and *Goodnight Moon* (1947), Marie Ets's *In the Forest* (1944), Charles Shaw's *It Looked Like Spilt Milk* (1947) and Esphyr Slobodkina's *Caps for Sale* (1947) have become classics. Publishers also began series, such as the *Read-to-Me* series of Thomas Y. Crowell, designed for use with young children in homes, nursery schools, and kindergartens.

Another noteworthy trend in the field of publishing during this decade was the rapid development of mass-market children's books. Publishers who had suspected there was an untapped preschool book market realized that this was indeed the case by 1943. Little Golden Books were introduced in the fall of 1942 as mass-market children's books. The first dozen or so featured stories written by respected authors such as Margaret Wise Brown and illustrated by popular artists; they were printed in a sturdy format and sold for 25 cents each. Picture books typically found in libraries cost several times that amount. By August 1943, Simon & Schuster had shipped 2,700,000 Little Golden Books to bookstores and had back orders for over 2 million more.[43] Many librarians saw some of these and most of the later mass-market books as inferior and felt an even greater desire to introduce quality books to preschoolers.

By the 1950s, library work with preschoolers was becoming a regular part of children's library service and not merely an

[43]James Cross Giblin, "Children's Book Publishing in America: 1919 to Now," *Children's Literature in Education* 17 (Fall 1986): 152.

auxiliary feature. One children's librarian felt that work with preschoolers had "doubled since World War II and if the comic and TV do no other good, they have led many a parent to the public library for an antidote."[44] Others suggested that the increase was due to the parents who had attended story hours and used the library extensively as children and who now brought their own children to the library "as soon as they could walk." The consequence was that the baby-boom produced "hordes of little children who invaded the library."[45]

The preschool story hour was being firmly established. In Elizabeth Gross's 1957 survey, 121 out of 259 libraries in communities of 35,000 people or more and 70 out of 303 libraries in smaller communities conducted preschool story hours. However, Gross indicated that librarians did not universally endorse the programs. She mentioned that some felt that the "play activities" included in story hours had no place in the library where the prime concern should be with books.[46] Nonetheless, those librarians who did offer the story hours were convinced of their value and proudly reported impressive statistics.[47]

As service for preschoolers was spreading across the U.S., it was also being reported in library literature in Britain, where one librarian urged her colleagues "not to miss" this important phase of children's library work. She argued that "in recent years increasing attention has been paid to the preschool child by

---

[44]Elizabeth Gross, "Trends in Library Service to Children," *Ohio Library Association Bulletin* 28 (October 1958): 9.

[45]Yolanda Federici, "History of Public Library Service to Children in Illinois," *Illinois Libraries* 50 (November 1968): 969.

[46]Elizabeth Gross and Gene I. Namoviez, *Children's Service in Public Libraries* (Chicago: American Library Association, 1963), 80.

[47]For example, "In a period covering twenty weeks in the spring and fall, we had an attendance of 8,241 preschool children and their mothers." Mary Tone, "Preschool Story Programs," *Library Journal* 78 (April 15, 1953): 674.

doctors, psychologists and religious bodies and it ill behoves [sic] the libraries as cultural institutions to ignore them." [48]

In this country, the fifties were also the time when the library felt the impact of the Public Library Inquiry,[49] the most extensive and competent study of the public library ever conducted.[50] The report of the study praised children's librarians and children's service but severely criticized other services. This gave children's librarians incentive to maintain the *status quo*, which meant continuing to offer preschool story hours.

From its inception, a minor debate about the preschool story hour was whether parents should be a part of the audience. A survey of the articles about this topic shows that a majority of libraries did not invite parents to join the group. For example, a librarian at the Detroit Public Library reasoned that the purpose of the story hours was not for the training of parents and argued that the "clinging" period for the preschooler was only prolonged when the parent was present.[51] Some librarians offered programs for mothers which were held simultaneously with story hours, while others, especially in smaller libraries with limited staff, asked parents to browse the shelves for material of interest.

A small number of libraries encouraged parents, usually mothers, to join the group. In these cases it was decided that the purpose of the story hour was also to introduce parents to picture books. Yet in other cases, librarians asked parents to join out of necessity. For example, Frances Clarke Sayers of the New York Public Library stated:

---

[48]S. Uniechowska, "Libraries and the Pre-school Child," *Library Association Record* 54 (November 1952): 364.

[49]Robert D. Leigh, *The Public Library in the United States* (New York: Columbia University Press, 1950).

[50]Patrick Williams, *The American Public Library and the Problem of Purpose* (Westport, Conn.: Greenwood Press, 1988), 65–66.

[51]Ethel C. Karrick, "The Preschool Story Hour," *ALA Bulletin* 41 (November 1947): 447.

At one of the branches the picture book hour reached such proportions that it became impossible to admit sixty-five or seventy children five years of age and under without the anchorage of their parents. So parents are now admitted. They sit in a solemn but responsive row in the back of the story hour room and explore with their children that rich contribution of American publishing, the world of picture books. This is a program in adult education.[52]

By the early 1960s, some librarians, to their credit, questioned the direction that the preschool story hour was taking: Was it truly a *library* function or could it as well be carried out by a nursery school or some other community agency? Was the preschool story hour a *library* program or just a program at the library? In re-evaluating the program, the librarians at the Gary Public Library in 1962 decided to make changes. They eliminated the use of the "flannelgraph" since they believed it served as a crutch for the storyteller rather than an aid to the child and acted as a barrier between the two. In addition, they encouraged librarians to focus attention on books and to lessen the prominence of records, finger plays, activity games, and puppets.[53]

Another event of the 1960s, which also reflects the question of content of the story hour, was the production of *The Pleasure Is Mutual: How to Conduct Effective Picture Book Programs*,[54] a film which was made using LSCA (Library Service and Construction Act) funds. It showed preschool story hours in action: groups of preschoolers watched as librarians read picture books. The film received critical acclaim. An important point made throughout

[52]Frances Clarke Sayers, "The Reading Program in the Children's Department," in *Youth, Communication and Libraries* ed. Frances Henne, Alice Brooks, and Ruth Ersted (Chicago: American Library Association, 1949), 128.

[53]Margaret Horner, "Pre-School Storytelling: A Reappraisal," *Wilson Library Bulletin* 37 (December 1962): 335–37.

[54]Westchester Library System of New York, *The Pleasure Is Mutual: How to Conduct Effective Picture Book Programs* 16mm, 24 min., color, sound, 1966, distributed by the Children's Book Council, New York.

the film and indicated by its subtitle is that story hours should focus primarily on picture books.

By the end of the sixties, service for preschoolers was receiving the lion's share of attention and time from children's librarians. The preschool story hour, or storytime as it was starting to be called since it avoided confusion about its duration, was the predominant type of preschool program. The following excerpt by Lowell Martin, a respected library administrator and educator, summarizes the library community's feeling about the story hour:

> The story hour [has been] one of the distinctive educational devices contributed by the public library.... Public libraries today have a decidedly larger portion of the children than of adults as regular readers. The program, though developed years ago, still has full vitality. It works in the slum as well as in the suburb. And in the public mind it is thought of as one of the most natural and significant activities of the public library.[55]

Development of Library Service for Parents of Preschoolers

The "adult education" movement in public libraries appeared and spread rapidly during the twenties and thirties. Its intention was to reach the more "purposeful" adult reader who was already or could be motivated to pursue his or her reading interests systematically.[56] One area of adult education was parent education which focused on parenthood and the study of the child.

Educational programs for parents existed sporadically outside libraries until the turn of the century, after which

---

[55]Lowell A. Martin, *Baltimore Reaches Out: Library Services to the Disadvantaged* (Baltimore: Enoch Pratt Free Library, 1967), 18.

[56]Margaret E. Monroe's *Library Adult Education: The Biography of an Idea* (Metuchen, N.J.: Scarecrow Press, 1963) is a history of the adult education movement.

organized parent education programs began. The growing child study movement of the 1920s influenced and paralleled the parent education movement,[57] and some librarians became attracted to the idea of helping to guide parents of children.

By the mid-1920s, many libraries were offering reading lists for parents. For example, the ALA Committee on Cooperation with the National Congress of Parents and Teachers irregularly published and widely distributed an annotated list titled *The Parents' Bookshelf.* The 1929 bibliography included citations of books and pamphlets on topics of play, and on psychological and physical development of young children.[58]

Materials for "study programs," which were even more in tune with the spirit of the adult education movement, were also compiled and published for parents. The "Reading with a Purpose" program was a popular one developed by the ALA. The thirty-eighth course in this series was *The Preschool Child: A Study Program to Accompany "The Young Child" by Bird T. Baldwin,* prepared by Grace Crum and published in 1929.[59] Crum describes the course in the book's preface:

> This study program, based on Bird T. Baldwin's reading course *The Young Child* and on the six books recommended in it, is prepared for the use of child study groups and individuals studying alone.
>
> As some study groups and parents at home will depend, perhaps, in part upon the city library for the books recommended, the lessons have been outlined with this plan in mind....

---

[57]Aline B. Auerback, *Trends and Techniques in Parent Education: A Critical Review* (New York: Child Study Association of America, 1961), 3–4.

[58]ALA Committee on Cooperation with the National Congress of Parents and Teachers, *The Parents' Bookshelf* (Chicago: American Library Association, 1929).

[59]Grace E. Crum, comp., *The Preschool Child: A Study Program to Accompany "The Young Child" by Bird T. Baldwin* Reading with a Purpose, No. 38 (Chicago: American Library Association, 1929).

The course is divided into twelve lessons such as The Development of the Senses, Play, Fear, Speech Development, The Parent-Child Relationship, and Mental Processes and Intelligence. Each lesson consists of a dozen or so questions (e.g., "Why should the child be allowed to experiment?" in the lesson on Play) followed by suggestions of topics for reports (e.g., "How I would tell the story of life to the preschool child" in the lesson on Mental Processes and Intelligence).

In many libraries, more comprehensive services for parents evolved from what was initially an attempt to disseminate bibliographies and study program materials. Lucille Stebbing described the pattern as follows:

> The first step most libraries take in this work is that of assembling the existing collection of parent education material in the one place most convenient for parents. Their ambition is to serve the parent who is already a member of the library and a reader of one sort or another. Some libraries have placed a book-rack near the charging desk, where the parental eye must rest while waiting to have other books stamped. Others have begun with a book-shelf in the Children's Room, since so many parents use the library only after their children [begin using it]....
>
> In the larger libraries these shelves soon expand into alcoves, or rooms for parents. Such rooms house the books, the magazines, the wealth of pamphlet material, and the many bibliographies pertaining to child training. Here also are the books that aim to educate the parent himself and to serve in molding the home as a proper environment for the child. Since a Parents' Room belongs to parents and others interested in children, it serves at various times as a lending library, a reading

room, a conference room, and a focal point for coordinating the community's reading in this field.[60]

By the mid-thirties, over a dozen public libraries had established the parent alcoves or rooms that Stebbing described.[61] The Youngstown (Ohio) Public Library's Mothers' Room, started in 1935, is the most famous of these, and its development has been chronicled elsewhere.[62] Nonetheless, two perceptive little books written by the founder of the Mothers' Room must be mentioned here.

In 1936 Clarence W. Sumner, director of the Youngstown Public Library, wrote *The Birthright of Babyhood* with an introduction by Garry C. Myers, head of the Department of Parent Education at Western Reserve University. Then in 1938 Garry C. Myers and Clarence W. Sumner together wrote *Books and Babies*.[63] The two books are similar in content: they describe the Mothers' Room in detail and "outline the best and surest method of instilling in the child a real and lasting love of books and reading that will carry through life." The advice they offer is remarkably advanced. For example:

A very important part of the child's training has been completed by the time he enters school. His education has been going on from the moment of his birth. It is in these early years that many permanent patterns of attitudes and habits have been forming. The little child not only is very impressionable, acquiring basic attitudes and habits, but his parents, being more impressionable

---

[60]Lucille R. Stebbing, "The Library and Parent Education," *Parent Education* 1 (January 1935): 3.

[61]William H. Bristow, "The Adult Education Program of the National Congress of Parents and Teachers," in *The Role of the Library in Adult Education* ed. by Louis R. Wilson (Chicago: University of Chicago Press, 1937), 96.

[62]Ann D. Carlson, *Early Childhood Literature Sharing Programs in Libraries* (Hamden, Conn.: Library Professional Publications, 1985).

[63]Clarence W. Sumner, *The Birthright of Babyhood* (New York: Thomas Nelson, 1936); and Garry C. Myers and Clarence W. Sumner, *Books and Babies* (Chicago: McClurg, 1938).

than they will be later, are also inclined to acquire
certain attitudes and habits toward the child which tend
to persist. Indeed, the parents' early attitude in respect
to parenthood may be just as significant as the early
attitudes which the child acquires.[64]

As the next excerpts make abundantly clear, Myers and
Sumner's ideas are remarkably in tune with those of the much
later emergent literacy movement:[65]

The program of introducing babies to books includes no
plan to teach little children to read before entering
school. On the contrary, the parent counselors of the
Mothers' Room take pain to warn parents not to try to
teach reading to the pre-school child.

The program aims at urging parents to continue reading
to the child at home for years after he has entered
school.... [Parents] will read to him from worthwhile
books that are beyond his own reading ability, thus
filling his mind with abundant facts and ideas and
cultivating his creative imagination. When this child,
between the ages of four and nine, wishes to dictate a
story of his own, his parents will readily record it for
him, preferably with a typewriter. After he has made
some progress in reading, he will delight in these
creations which have been neatly copied for him.
Meanwhile this child, who from his very early years has
listened to the members of his family read to him, will
have acquired a powerful urge to read alone.

Psychologists tell us that the child [who is] read to a
great deal before entering school will never become a
mere word reader. Words have for months and years
conveyed rich meaning to him. The pictures which he
watched as he listened have enriched this meaning. He

---

[64]Myers, *Books and Babies*, 9.

[65]A discussion of emergent literacy development is offered in
Chapter 3.

has associated these meanings and fruitful imagery they brought forth not with the one reading so much as with the book. The powerful association of pictured stories with the printed page has been built for him, and the longing for the ability to acquire this meaning from the printed page alone has increased.[66]

It is evident from reports and articles appearing in the literature that there was a small but vocal group of librarians, most of whom were not children's librarians, who strongly believed in the value of parents' rooms and the vital role the public library played in parent education. A speech given at the 1939 ALA conference reflects these convictions:

> We all need to realize that parents are the only permanent factors in the education of any individual. Parents affect each individual from the moment of conception and throughout life. What parents do, or do not do, is so important that we have to realize that to aid a parent is as important as to aid a child, because the parent is in a position to nullify or to fortify the efforts of professional workers. No matter how excellent a teacher or a librarian may be, the opportunity to serve any particular child is temporary. I do not mean, of course, that there should be a diminution of effort in behalf of children, but that each one of us should widen our sympathies, as well as our information, to include parents.[67]

The forties began with a White House Conference on "Children in Democracy." Its report recognized the roles that parent education and children's service played. The report recommended: "Libraries should provide for special collections and personnel to serve children. Provisions should also be made for

---

[66]Ibid., 96–98.

[67]Gertrude Laws, "Report of the Joint Parent Education Committee of the ALA and the National Conference on Parent Education, San Francisco ALA Conference, 1939," *ALA Bulletin* 33 (October 15, 1939): 146.

material and for advisory service for parents on subjects relating to child care and training."[68]

After World War II, Elizabeth M. Smith presented the results of a survey on parent education in libraries to the First Postwar National Parent Education Conference at Atlantic City in 1946. The survey Smith conducted sounds rather informal: she "corresponded" with 94 libraries from thirty-one states. Her results showed that in spite of decimated staffs, there had been marked progress in the library's contribution to parent education since 1937: "Promising new experiments have been made, activities well started have not been allowed to drop, and ... a greater understanding and appreciation of service for parents and its requirements [can be sensed]."[69]

From the information gleaned from her correspondence, Smith concluded that "parents shelves, talks to groups on books and library resources, book exhibits at meetings, and the making of reading lists and bibliographies" are the generally accepted activities. She also developed a composite picture of work with and for parents in a library. Smith's idealized composite library has a special department of "Family Living" which is headed by a librarian trained in child psychology, parent education, and children's literature; it has a collection which

> covers child care, development and health, family living, marriage, mental hygiene, homemaking including such homemaking guides as books of games, storytelling and stories to read aloud. It includes also a bridge to the children's department in the form of a model children's library which puts special stress on books for the pre-school child.[70]

---

[68]U.S. Children's Bureau, *General Report of the White House Conference on Children in a Democracy* (Washington, D.C.: U.S. Government Printing Office, 1940), 42.

[69]Elizabeth M. Smith, "The Public Library Contributes to Parent Education," *Library Journal* 71 (October 15, 1946): 1427.

[70]Ibid., 1428.

The Family Living department staff works with groups and group leaders and offers services in "the guidance in the use of books." The library staff also goes out into the field with its books. It gives advisory service to individual parents. Smith points out that "educating parents in children's literature and the cultivating of a child's reading taste have been responsibilities of libraries for many years" and librarians rightly continue to value it since they "see so much that is good come out of a child's well-guided reading."

There is no record in the literature of any examples of the Family Living department as envisioned by Smith. Furthermore, Parents' and Mothers' Rooms, which had had strong support from several communities and thrived along with the parent education movement of the thirties, by and large disappeared soon after the war.[71] One could speculate that these comprehensive programs were eliminated to make way for the popular preschool story hour.

Library literature on the subject from the mid-forties to the late-fifties consisted of Smith's article and a handful of others. A few were about parent education programs such as Virginia Summers's program that began in 1947 and "offered the mothers of Lansing a chance to learn something about the psychology of the young child and something about child education generally."[72] Other articles were about the parent-preschool child story hour which contained a deliberate parent-training component.[73]

---

[71]*Library Literature* dropped the "Mothers' Rooms" subject heading in 1942. It should be noted that a few survived thanks to the conviction of the individual library director. The Parents' Room of the Mount Vernon (New York) Public Library was one such holdout described by Eleanor Phinney in *Library Adult Education in Action* (Chicago: American Library Association, 1956), 29–31.

[72]Virginia Summers, "For Mothers of Preschool Children," *Wilson Library Bulletin* 23 (April 1949): 623.

[73]For example, Mary O. Condit's "Story Hour Attracts Mothers," *Library Journal* 71 (September 1, 1946): 1112–3; and Gladys Young's "The Child-Parent Hour at the Kirkwood [Missouri] Public Library," *MLA Quarterly* 19 (September 1958): 87–88.

Even though the comprehensive programs were gone, most children's librarians continued to be active in less ambitious service to parents. More limited programs for them were playing a definite part in library service to children during the fifties. Harriet Long discusses the typical kinds of service during this period.

> In relation to the child's reading, the children's librarian has traditionally realized the importance of the parent's interest. Suggesting books for reading aloud within the family circle; advising the parent about certain titles which may help his child to meet a behavior or emotional problem; talks to Parent-Teacher Association groups; and series of lectures on children's literature to mothers' clubs are common paths of service.[74]

The 1960s were much like the 1950s in that there was a continued but not substantial interest in parent education in the library community. There were, however, calls for action.

The 1961 ALA Conference in Cleveland included a pre-conference meeting on "The Adult and the Child's World: The Library's Potential for Service" sponsored by the Adult Services Division and the Children's Services Division of the ALA. At the meeting, Jewel Drickamer addressed the topic of serving children through adults and asked: "The degree to which library service to children has been developed is one of the real achievements of American librarianship. But have we really explored *all* the avenues? Is there a tremendous untapped future ahead of us in which we might extend our services to yet more children *through adults*?"[75] Ruth Warncke echoed the call two years later and described three typical types of services for parents: (1) organized series of group meetings for the mothers of preschoolers attending story hours, (2) workshops designed to teach storytelling techniques to library volunteers and those

---

[74]Harriet G. Long, *Rich the Treasure: Public Library Service to Children* (Chicago: American Library Association, 1953), 52.

[75]Jewel Drickamer, "Serving Children through Adults," *Library Journal* 87 (March 15, 1962): 1079.

"who work with children in many situations," and (3) collections of books and pamphlets on child development housed in children's departments.[76]

In the mid-1960s the U.S. turned its attention to the plight of the poor. Evaluation of the federal War on Poverty programs, such as Head Start and Follow Through, led educational policy makers to conclude that involvement of the parents helped reinforce the effects of the program while it was in operation and sustained them after the program ended.[77] Lowell Martin endorsed the idea of parent involvement in his 1967 Baltimore study where he advocated parent education and participation, especially in the case of disadvantaged preschoolers:

> Programs for this early age must break new ground, differing from customary methods of both schools and libraries, and should rest upon knowledge of the psychology of early childhood development. They will be more promising if parents can be involved with their children.[78]

In the early 1970s, an evaluative study appeared that supported Martin's conviction. After analyzing the relationship between program characteristics and program effectiveness, *A Study of Exemplary Public Library Reading and Reading-Related Programs for Children, Youth, and Adults* concluded that "preschool programs which provide activities for both preschool children and their mothers scored higher on the effectiveness measure than programs limited to preschool children."[79]

---

[76]Ruth Warncke, "Public Library Services to Adults Working with Children," *Library Trends* 12 (July 1963): 84–91.

[77]A more detailed description of these programs is offered in Chapter 2.

[78]Lowell A. Martin, *Baltimore Reaches Out: Library Service to the Disadvantaged* (Baltimore: Enoch Pratt Free Library, 1967), 36.

[79]Barss, Reitzel & Associates, Inc. *A Study of Exemplary Public Library Reading and Reading-Related Programs for Children, Youth, and Adults* Vol. I (Prepared for the Office of Education, U.S. Dept of Health, Education, and Welfare) (Cambridge, Mass.:Barss, Reitzel & Associates, Inc., 1972), 10.

The new nationwide recognition of the parents' role in influencing the development of their preschoolers appeared in both the scholarly and the popular press during the seventies. Books, magazines, newspaper columns, parent and child play groups, and parent discussion groups designed for parent education seemed to sprout everywhere. Librarians, too, joined in.

The late-1970s signaled a re-awakening period for librarians as they recognized the potential of public library service to preschoolers through their parents. As librarians moved toward this larger role in parent education, they attempted to reach organized groups of parents, not just the individual parent as they had done in the past. They often sought out opportunities to talk to groups of parents, such as AAUW, church groups, Rotary, etc.[80] In other cases, librarians initiated dozens of comprehensive parent education programs, often using LSCA and other grant funds and sporting catchy names such as "Good Start" and "Giant Step" of the Glassboro (New Jersey) Public Library, "Project Little Kids" of the Greenville (South Carolina) Public Library, "P.E.P." (Parent Education Program) of the Westchester (New York) Library System, or "Project Leapfrog" of the Phillipsburg (New Jersey) Public Library.

By the 1980s, service for parents of preschoolers was firmly established and played a significant role in many public libraries. As one librarian said: "Parent education programs and services are ... no luxury in the public library. They are a top priority necessary to reach the ultimate goal of making lifelong readers and library users of every child."[81]

Development of Library Service for Teachers and Caregivers of Preschoolers

Serving preschoolers through their teachers in preschools and caregivers in child care centers is based on the desire to reach a

---

[80]Faith Hektoen, "Parent Support Programs," *PLA Newsletter* 16 (Winter 1977): 16.

[81]Gail Terwilliger, "A Sampling of Parent Education Programs," *Public Libraries* 23 (Summer 1984): 54.

greater number of young children. Since preschoolers who attend early childhood programs often spend a large portion of their waking hours with their teachers and caregivers, it makes sense for children's librarians to provide service to the adults who work with young children. Teachers and caregivers who spend time with large numbers of children afford librarians great leverage in reaching young children. Another advantage of programs for teachers and caregivers is the ability to involve otherwise hard-to-reach children since preschoolers are unlikely to come to the library unless they are brought by their parents, and it is those whose parents are least likely to bring them who may derive the most benefit from the books in the library.

One of the earliest reports of service for child care centers appeared in *Library Journal* in 1945.[82] Even though service was provided by the library section of the school system and not by the public library, it is worth mentioning the article for historical purposes. Jean Cook, the author and former public librarian, describes how, during World War II, the need for working women forced a tremendous growth of child care facilities in Los Angeles.[83] She gives fascinating descriptions of the facilities and daily activities of the centers that operate "for a charge of fifty cents a day." When the supervisors of the centers realized they should have a collection of picture books to be used with the children, they asked for help from the Library and Textbook Section of the City Schools. Cook's description of the way rotating book collections were developed and of how books were selected for the collections anticipates practices that public libraries would follow thirty years later.

Up until the late 1960s, there were no reports of public library service to nursery schools and child care centers in the literature. Of course there may be instances of such service that

---

[82]Jean G. Cook, "Books for Nursery Schools," *Library Journal* 70 (January 1, 1945): 18–20.

[83]Under the Lanham Act, the federal government established child care facilities in most centers of war industry. A discussion of child care facilties is offered in Chapter 2.

went unchronicled. One could speculate that libraries which offered preschool story hours may have offered these for preschoolers in nursery schools and child care. Minnie Fuller's statement in her unpublished dissertation supports this:

> Although the pre-school story hour programs are aimed at the children who do not attend the nursery schools, these same services are rendered to the various nursery schools that make appointments during the week. The teachers bring these children instead of the parents.[84]

It is not surprising that public libraries did not serve teachers and caregivers of preschoolers before the late 60s when one considers how few nursery schools and child care centers there were. As will be discussed in Chapter 2, a 1932 Department of Education survey reported locating only 202 nursery schools. The many Lanham Act centers which sprung up during World War II closed after women were no longer needed in war industries. The argument against early childhood programs as "the enemy of family life" heard during the 50s and 60s greatly slowed the growth of the nursery school movement and may have even predisposed some libraries to feel that such service was "un-American." However, as more middle class and divorced women with young children sought jobs during the late 60s and early 70s, an increasing number of nursery schools and child care centers appeared to meet their needs, and a change of attitude by the public also occurred.

As the number of nursery schools and child care centers grew, some librarians, especially in urban areas, began initiating services, in large measure using LSCA funds. One of the first libraries to report service to teachers and caregivers was the Brooklyn Public Library. Suzanne Glazer describes the service which brought preschool story hours to church- and privately-run child care centers, Head Start programs, housing projects, and community centers. From February through September

---

[84]Minnie N. Fuller, "The Public Library and the Pre-School Child" (M.S.L.S. thesis, Catholic University, 1963), 3.

1965, the sixteen aides who were trained by the librarians and were familiar with the community conducted 2,272 story hours for 33,664 preschoolers.[85]

By the early 1970s, an increasing number of libraries had developed programs. Two noteworthy ones are The Early Childhood Education Project (ECEP) for adults working with children aged two to five, which was developed by the San Francisco Public Library, and the Sharing Literature with Children program where children's librarians trained adults, especially child care center personnel, in literature-sharing techniques, which was developed by the Orlando Public Library.[86]

By the end of the seventies, service for teachers and caregivers of preschoolers was solidly established in many libraries throughout this country. A wide variety of activities were reported in the literature. In addition to the grant-funded comprehensive projects, many libraries initiated less ambitious activities. The four most typical ones were (1) collections of books loaned to preschools and child care centers, (2) theme-related storytime kits loaned to adults who work with groups of children, (3) workshops conducted by children's librarians to train preschool teachers and child care personnel in literature-sharing techniques, and (4) storytimes for preschoolers conducted by children's librarians at preschools, child care centers, or libraries.[87]

---

[85]Suzanne Glazer, "Who's Nonverbal?: Brooklyn Public Library's Preschool Program," *Library Journal* 91 (January 15, 1966): 341–43.

[86]Details of the programs are in Binnie L. Tate's *The Role of the Public Library as an Alternative Force in Early Childhood Education* (Washington, D.C.: U.S. Office of Education, 1974; Carol [sic] Sue Peterson, "Sharing Literature with Children," in *Start Early for an Early Start*, ed Ferne Johnson (Chicago: American Library Association, 1976); and "San Francisco Develops Early Childhood Ed Center," *School Library Journal* 19 (December 1972): 8.

[87]Frances A. Smardo, an authority on early childhood programs in libraries, describes many recent activities in "Public Library Services for Young Children in Day Care and Their Caregivers," *Public Library Quarterly* 7 (Spring/Summer 1986): 45–56.

A History of Early Childhood Programs

Beginnings and Early Influences

CARE AND EDUCATION of young children outside the home has a long history. In his *Republic,* Plato advocated it in ancient Greece, and the Romans provided public child care for their citizens. During the 17th to 19th centuries, Comenius, Rousseau, Pestalozzi, Robert Owen, among others, proposed schools for young children as a way of improving social conditions. Although the reformers of the 17th to 19th centuries were guided by different philosophies and religious beliefs, some of their principles and methods continue to influence early childhood programs today.

The emphasis of Johann Amos Comenius (1592–1670), the last bishop of the Moravian Brethren, on health care and his suggestions for making the child's world intelligible to him are accepted tenets in early childhood education. His belief that a curriculum should be based on the child's experiences is also accepted today.

The ideas of French philosopher Jean Jacques Rousseau (1712–1778) that children are not little adults, and that a child should be studied before he is "cultivated" preceeded the common current practice of the observational method.

The ideas of Johann "Papa" Pestalozzi (1746–1827), an Italian-Swiss educator, startled the eighteenth century world.

His idea that teaching methods must be adjusted to children's stages of development, which he termed a "process of unfolding," is a cornerstone of today's programs. Furthermore, his belief that the impression of things should precede verbal instruction, and that children should use their senses and learn from doing is implicit in current early childhood programs. Pestalozzi's rejection of the rote learning of the alphabet, which he called the "first plague of youth—the miserable letters," was years ahead of his contemporaries' practices.

Robert Owen (1771–1858), a socialist who believed that the fate of a man depended "not upon his original nature but upon the environment in which society placed him,"[1] began a school in Scotland in 1816 for the one- to six-year-old children of workers in his cotton mill. His opposition to book learning for young children and his belief that children should be taught by surrounding them with good role models continues to be a part of programs today.

Later pioneers such as Maria Montessori in Italy, the McMillan sisters and Grace Owen in England, and Patty Smith Hill in America who created the modern nursery school were deeply influenced by these early reformers.

Montessori Method and Schools

The eponymous Maria Montessori[2] (1870–1952) was an Italian physician, professor, and educator. She was the first woman in Italy to receive a medical degree. During her studies she became interested in the work of two distinguished doctors, Itard and Seguin. Itard (1775–1838), physician to the National Institution for the Deaf and Dumb in Paris, is best known for his experimental treatment of the Wild Boy of Aveyron. Edouard Seguin (1812–1880), who studied Itard's work, is remembered as

---

[1]Ilse Forest, *The School for the Child from Two to Eight* (New York: Ginn, 1935), 39.

[2]E.M. Standing, *Maria Montessori: Her Life and Work* (London: Hollis and Carter, 1957), 3–68.

an educator who developed materials for use in teaching retarded children.[3]

Using materials and methods derived from Seguin's,
Montessori began her work with a group of retarded children in
Rome. Success with these children led her to believe that normal
children could also benefit from her methods. The opportunity
came in 1907 when she began classes with slum children from
two to six years of age. She called her school *Casa dei Bambini.*

Montessori based her methods on the theory that children
could learn easily when given the freedom to progress at their
own rate in a well organized environment that offered tasks
suited to their level of development. Her "prepared environments" provided preschoolers with attractive, spacious rooms
with furniture scaled to child size (which she is credited with
developing), and with the "didactic materials" laid out neatly on
easily accessible shelves.

Her curriculum was organized around several "periods" in
the child's development, each of which had its particular
requirement for interaction with the environment. During the
period of the "absorbent mind", from birth to six years of age,
and most especially in the substage of "greatest sensitivity and
receptivity", from three to six years of age, the curriculum
engaged the children in exercises of practical life, motor
education, sensory education, intellectual education, language
education, and the teaching of reading, writing, and numeration.
Children from two to six years of age were grouped together so
that older children could assist and serve as models for younger
ones.[4]

The role of the teacher, or the "directress" as Montessori
preferred to call her, was to serve as a guide—a skilled, im-
personal observer who could determine when the child was

---

[3]Robert John Fynne, *Montessori and Her Inspirers* (London:
Longmans, Green, 1924).

[4]Maria Montessori, *The Montessori Method* (New York: Schocken,
1964).

ready to move to more sophisticated tasks. Importance was placed not between the child and teacher but between the child and materials. Montessori believed that the environment would allow the child to manifest his or her developing competencies without adult interference. Therefore, the role of the school was to create an environment that would teach the child with a minimum of adult intervention. Freedom of movement in these prepared environments was a hallmark of the method.[5]

The Montessori movement spread throughout the world. Schools were established in several places in the U.S. between 1910 and 1920. Montessori described the origins, principles, methods, and results of her pedagogy in a 1909 book which was subsequently translated into English as *The Montessori Method* in 1912 and which immediately became a best-seller. Kits of the didactic apparatus became available for home use from a New York manufacturer in 1912.

Most of the American schools, however, disappeared during the 1920s through the 1950s, either closing or becoming nursery schools not unlike others around them. In the 1960s a resurgence occurred in the U.S.; Montessori schools as well as training programs for teachers were reestablished. Some of the training programs adhered to Maria Montessori's regimen while others modified the activities to include those not found in her writings, such as block-building, or even those she considered not admissible, such as dramatic play activities.[6]

---

[5]Maria Montessori, *The Child in the Family* (New York: Avon, 1970), 61–131.

[6]It is interesting to note that Montessori had serious objections to the practice of encouraging young children to use their imaginations in make-believe play. She emphasized the importance of "occupations" in which behavior had to be adapted to reality. In fact, Montessori materials present the child with a problem in adaptive behavior. For example, the child has to fit different sized cylinders into corresponding holes, or to arrange insets in their places, or to grade color shades in a series. Montessori viewed make-believe as an escape from reality, which needed to be discouraged in the interest of "intellectual efficiency". She considered it essentially dishonest because in talking about stories

Nursery Schools in England

The first nursery schools in England were founded by Rachel and Margaret McMillan, health clinic workers who worked with underprivileged children. Their work was supported by the Medical Inspection of Children Act of 1907, which was initiated because of the discovery that recruits for the Boer War were in poor physical condition. This bill focused attention on the need for better medical care of young children and led the English Board of Education in 1908 to offer funds for establishing facilities for the care for young children.[7]

Rachel and Margaret McMillan took up the challenge and established a nursery school in 1909 in "a very poor, very crowded" district in the south-east of London. At the clinic, the sisters saw and cured thousands of children suffering from diseases only to have the diseases return, since "the clinic, as such, cannot make any kind of war with the causes that breed these diseases." On the other hand, the nursery school, "if properly equipped, would cut at the root of all this misery. It would bring up a race of children with new habits and new needs."[8]

The sisters believed that the nursery school should function as a preventive for children's mental and physical illnesses that were so prevalent in the slums. The basic philosophy was based on the supposition that "children need that very important kind of early education called *Nurture*."[9] The McMillans conceived of nurturance as dealing with the whole child. Rachel's axiom was: "Educate every child as if he were your own."[10]

---

involving witches and ogres or talking animals, children were being presented with a false picture of reality.

[7]Catherine Landreth, *Education of the Young Child* (New York: John Wiley, 1942), 5.

[8]Margaret McMillan, *The Nursery School* (London: J.M. Dent, 1921), 25.

[9]Ibid., 22.

[10]Ibid., 11.

The first schools were single-story buildings with large doorways or French windows which opened into gardens and large play areas. The children moved freely between indoors and outdoors in these settings. Gardens were planted in the schools, and herbs were grown to provide sensory experiences.

Like Montessori, the McMillans' educational program was influenced by Edouard Seguin (1812–1880), the French doctor and educator who found refuge in America after Louis Napoleon became powerful.[11] With great fervor, Margaret draws a parallel between Seguin's and her missions:

> Edouard Seguin was a teacher of defective children and a follower of Pinel, Itard and Esquirol. Absorbed in the great task of drawing the idiot and the imbecile from the abyss in which they are plunged, he was led by his toil for these to lay bare and expose many of the processes whereby human beings are prepared for a human destiny. Near the teeming ports of the New World he saw the exiles of poverty, of tyranny, and of despair arrive from every European country, and having been faithful to the poor idiot, he had a gift in his hand for this new world. We also hope we have a gift for the millions who are not idiots, not sub-normal, but who are yet driven back from the outgoing life of civilised humanity by the poverty or rigour of their lives.[12]

Margaret McMillan outlined her educational program in *The Nursery School*, published in 1919, reprinted in 1921, and revised in 1930. This book contains sound ideas for educators today. McMillan saw both the home and the community as contributors to the education of young children. She believed that the first few years of life in children's development were of "supreme importance", arguing that love and security were as vital to the child's overall progress as material well-being. She stated that if

---

[11]Mabel E. Talbot, *Edouard Seguin* (New York: Bureau of Publications, Teachers College, Columbia University, 1964), 11.
[12]Ibid., 13.

her educational program was to have any impact, parents must be involved in their children's education. Schools alone could not overcome the ills of society, and parents must be helped to improve their child-rearing practices.

Learning activities were outlined which differed by age levels. Three- and four-year-old children were expected to wash themselves, tie their shoelaces, and care for plants and animals such as rabbits and birds. A strong emphasis was placed on cleaning, such as picking up "waste paper and rubbish that spoils the order of the place," and sweeping. Activities involving music, rhythm, and language were emphasized to develop the senses. Free play activities with water and sand were also included.

Unlike Maria Montessori, Margaret McMillan placed high value on the education of the imagination. She emphasizes it in a 1924 publication, *Education through the Imagination.* She saw expressive activity, play, art, and movement as imitative but good preparation for later life. She felt that imagination grew naturally in children during the early years, and could be used to provide a framework for an "organic" form of education.[13]

Facilities for the nursery schools included small tables used by the children for activities. There were play houses, specimen cupboards, and low shelves holding "things on such a level that little people can handle them and dust them." The teacher's role was to recognize "teachable moments" and intervene at the appropriate time.

Strong emphasis was placed on the children being outdoors. Some schools became known as Open-Air Nursery Schools. Margaret McMillan claimed: "To move, to run, to find things out by new movement, to feel one's life in every limb, that is the life of early childhood."[14] In her writings, she refers to parks as

---

[13]Margaret McMillan, *Education through the Imagination* (New York: D. Appleton, 1924), 9–15.

[14]Margaret McMillan, *The Nursery School* (London: J.M. Dent, 1921), 27.

"great open spaces that are the lungs of a district," and to "earth, sun, air, sleep and joy" as the great healers. Indeed, she likens the nursery school to "the human garden that may blossom in the slum."[15]

It is curious to note that the educational movement in England during this period often used analogies similar to those of McMillan. This may have reflected the belief that education could take place only in an environment that protected the health and welfare of the child. For example, Lillian de Lissa, principal of Gipsy Hill Training College in London, suggested that the environment of a nursery school dictates that teachers be gardeners of a type:

> Just as a gardener digs into the soil the requirements of the plants, so the school should surround the child with the means of growth, and in this carefully prepared environment it should be left to grow with the same freedom as the plants. Teachers, like gardeners, must be the servants of Nature, not her masters; their work is to discover Nature's purpose and help the organism to work in harmony with it.[16]

Another nursery school pioneer in England was Grace Owen of Manchester who edited and wrote most of the chapters of *Nursery School Education*, which, like McMillan's book, had a great impact on the movement and helped to extend it throughout Europe and to the United States. Owen viewed the responsibility of the nursery school as four-fold. First, it must provide the right conditions for free and healthy physical development, including such things as open air, space to run about, and rooms "having a sunny aspect." Second, it must provide a stimulating environment since the years between two and six are a time when the child is "gathering ideas from his

---

[15]Margaret McMillan, *Education through the Imagination* (New York: D. Appleton, 1924), 12–59.

[16]Foster Watson, ed. *The Encyclopaedia and Dictionary of Education* (London: Sir Isaac Pitman, 1922), s.v. "Nursery Schools," by Lillian de Lissa.

surroundings with amazing rapidity ... his mind is constantly occupied with things present to the senses, and he receives multitudes of vivid impressions, the material for later thinking." Third, it must provide the child with the means and opportunity to "express his own ideas and feelings, to help him to acquire more skill as he feels the need of it, and to supply an atmosphere of love and sympathy." And finally, it must provide for the development of social relationships.[17]

There were many similarities between the McMillans' and Grace Owen's goals for their schools. However, one difference between their curricula stands out. Owen rejected formal instruction of any type for children under age six, reasoning that the child "is fully occupied in the mind and body with learning from actual experience." The McMillans, on the other hand, advocated the introduction of reading, writing, and number lessons if the child showed an interest.

Conditions created by World War I added fresh incentive to the nursery school movement since children of women workers needed care. Moreover, a renewed need for "mental hygiene" became apparent from data gathered in war hospitals. Many of the mental and emotional abnormalities of the veterans could be traced directly to a lack of good mental hygiene at home and at school during early childhood.

The work of the McMillans and Grace Owen became increasingly successful, and more nursery schools were opened throughout the slums of the larger industrial cities in England. One such school was opened in August 1917 by Mr. H.A.L. Fisher, Minister of Education. The school was dedicated to Rachel McMillan who, according to Margaret, "poured forth all her resources, material and also spiritual, in order to begin and develop this work, and who died exhausted and alas! perhaps saddened by the long fight, on her birthday, Lady Day, 1917, just

---

[17]Grace Owen, ed., *Nursery School Education* (New York: Dutton, 1920), 22–24.

as the plans for the extension of our Nursery Centre were passed."[18]

In 1918, the Fisher Act was passed and provided that nursery schools be part of the national school system in districts where parents could not provide adequate care for their young children. Great was the need for these centers. Miss E. Stevinson, Superintendent of the Rachel McMillan Open-Air School, gives a vivid account of her particular school and the situations the children came from:

> Mrs. Taylor is carrying her baby carefully wrapped in a large shawl. She folds back one corner of the wrap and discloses the small pale face of a little girl, apparently about three years old. Glancing nervously at the Superintendent:

> "She *can* walk, Miss," she says, hurriedly. "On'y give 'er the back of a chair to 'old to and she can get along beautiful. She's a real strong child is our Edith May tho' she mayn't look it. It's all along of 'er 'avin' been tied to the table that's made 'er weak on 'er pins." The little mite inside the shawl sits up and protests, feebly crying. Her mother hushes her tenderly. "She don't cry often, Nurse. She's a real good child, but she ain't used to folks."

> "Do you go out to work?" asks the Superintendent, as she takes down particulars of the child's age and address.

> "Why, yes, Miss. There's on'y me *to* work. 'Er father's dead. Mrs. Mason, me neighbour, she's minded Edith May till now. But ever since the kiddie got burned Mrs. Mason's nervous like, and so whenever she's busy she takes and ties 'er up to the table leg. 'Arf a crown a week I pay 'er to keep Edith May. But it seems as if the babby oughter be walkin' now, and, Miss, it'd be a godsend if I

---

[18]Margaret McMillan, *The Nursery School* (London: J.M. Dent, 1921), 24.

could get 'er in 'ere, so it would." And the mother's anxious eyes follow the sturdy little figures of our toddlers as they trot to and fro along the garden paths.

"I'd like our Edith May to get a bit er colour in 'er cheeks and to run like them," she says wistfully. "She don't know what a garden is, poor mite."

Feebly protesting, little Edith May is carried to the Toddlers' Shelter. The mother kisses her and hurries away, waving her hand in farewell; and at that moment Edith May doubtless longs for the familiar table leg. But she is soon consoled, and her anxious little mother, peeping round the corner ten minutes later, sees her happily hugging a Teddy bear and watching the nurse ladle hot porridge into rows of waiting basins.[19]

By all accounts, the nursery schools in England served their purpose. The preschoolers grew healthy and strong and learned "proper physical and mental hygiene." As evidence of good preventive care, Stevinson describes the case when an influenza epidemic occurred during the winter of 1921 in south-east London. There were no deaths and no cases of serious illness among the school children, while children who did not attend the school "died in great numbers."[20] The Fisher Act of 1918 which allowed for matching funds needed to establish these programs also attests to success of the McMillans' work.

Unfortunately, funds at the local level were not forthcoming in the post-war economic depression and the expansion of the nursery school movement in England slowed. Nevertheless, the movement, which started initially as a public health concern but soon incorporated a solid educational base, established principles that later influenced movements throughout the world.

---

[19]E. Stevinson, *The Open-Air Nursery School* (London: J. M. Dent, 1923), 2–3.
[20]Ibid., 60.

When comparing the Montessori schools with the English nursery schools, one finds common elements. The schools were established to help the slum children of cities, were influenced by the work of Seguin, and incorporated sensory education into their programs. However, the English nursery school assumed more responsibility for physical, emotional, and social development and for working with parents. The freedom from a specific method also allowed English nursery schools to develop more diverse and flexible programs which responded to new educational thinking and social situations.

Nursery Schools in the United States

The decade of the 1920s saw the emergence of the nursery school movement in this country. The pioneers of the movement in England helped lay the foundation here. Dr. Patty Smith Hill of Columbia University's Teachers College was a leader who did much to establish early childhood education programs. In her foreword to the American edition of Margaret McMillan's *The Nursery School*, she claimed that "At last the world seems to be awakening to the fact that human destiny is largely shaped by the nurture or neglect of early infancy and childhood."[21] She announced that children of The McMillans' school "not only live but have a rich abundant life of health, and happiness, and beauty which should be the birthright of *all the children of all nations and races;*" and she credited the McMillans, Grace Owen, and others for "saving and educating the babies of England."[22]

Through Hill's influence, Grace Owen was brought to lecture at Teachers College. Many trained "nurse-teachers" from England were also brought to work in the university-based nursery schools which were being established. Thanks to this academic nexus the American movement was brought into close contact with the English movement with its well organized plans and with its provision for "physical and mental hygiene."

---

[21]Margaret McMillan, *The Nursery School* (London: J.M. Dent, 1921), v.

[22]Ibid., x–xi.

However, in this country the movement originated from a diverse set of social interests and purposes, not solely from the philanthropic purpose of providing health care to the children of the slums. Therefore, the U.S. movement proceeded along several different lines, each with its own purpose and organization. For example, there were the research-center nursery schools which began in the early twenties, many of which were made possible through grants from the Laura Spelman Rockefeller Memorial, including those at Columbia University, Yale, and the State Universities of Minnesota, California, and Iowa. These were organized to furnish laboratories for the study of "normal" young children.

There were also nursery schools which were organized as a part of training programs in home economics. These included the one established at the Merrill-Palmer School of Motherhood and Home Training in Detroit in 1922 for students of home economics; the school at Vassar which was established in 1926 by alumnae demands to give students an opportunity to learn more about children and homemaking; and those at several universities and state teachers' colleges set up to train future teachers.

In addition, there were the cooperative nursery schools, such as the one begun in 1915 at the University of Chicago by faculty wives in order to provide social play for their preschoolers, and the one established at Smith College begun in 1926 by the Institute for the Coordination of Women's Interests. There were also the philanthropic nursery schools, similar in purpose to the McMillans', found in settlement houses, women's prisons, and poverty areas in the U.S. Finally, private nursery schools appeared and gradually increased in number to meet the demands of mothers, many of whom read or heard about the advantages of the university-centered schools.

It is evident from this diversity that the American nursery school developed very differently from the English institution. Unlike the schools in England, they were not restricted to lower social and economic groups. Nursery schools in the U.S. served the purposes of research, parent and teacher education, and assistance to working parents. It is also important to note that despite the diversity of types of nursery schools in the U.S. at the end of the 1920s, the total number was still relatively low. In 1932, the Department of Education conducted a survey and reported locating only 202 nursery schools.[23]

It became clear during this period of development that trained personnel were needed to carry on nursery school work. The questions of what training would be most desirable and what standards should be required of nursery teachers and schools were subjects of great debate between 1926 and 1928. At this time the National Association for Nursery Education was organized which addressed these questions.[24] The eighteen initial members included such prestigious and forward thinkers as Arnold Gesell of the Yale Psycho Clinic, May Hill (Arbuthnot) of Western Reserve University, Patty Smith Hill of Teachers College, Mary Dabney Davis of the U.S. Office of Education, Harriet Johnson of the Bureau of Educational Experiments (later to be called the Bank Street College of Education), and Rose Alschuler of Winnetka Public School Nursery Unit. It is not surprising that the excellent documents these committees produced provided clear direction to the movement.

In the foreword to one document, *Minimum Essentials for Nursery School Education* of 1929, Lois Hayden Meeks of Teachers College states that the movement "is directly related to other movements which are themselves new, unformed, rapidly changing: mental hygiene, child development, parent education, home economics' emphasis on child care, and the changing place of women in the home and society." She describes the formation of the Association as "a direct outgrowth of the desire of the specialists in nursery school education to keep a critical attitude toward the movement, to protect it from propagation at the hand

---

[23]Catherine Landreth, *Education of the Young Child* (New York: John Wiley, 1942), 10.

[24]Ilse Forest, *The School for the Child from Two to Eight* (New York: Ginn, 1935), 48.

of untrained enthusiasts, and to encourage an experimental, open-minded attitude towards the development of new programs, techniques and organization."[25]

The Depression of the 1930s had a great impact on the development of nursery schools. With widespread unemployment and decreased tax revenues, school districts did away with many teaching posts they no longer could afford. In October 1933, the federal government under the Federal Emergency Relief Administration authorized the establishment of Federal Emergency Nursery Schools whose purpose was "to provide employment for unemployed teachers, to foster the physical, mental, and social well-being of young children, and to promote better morale among their parents." [26] A short time later, the government provided funds under the Works Projects Administration for nursery schools. The establishment of schools was directed by local school districts with major problems arising from hastily trained staff, ill-equipped buildings, and deficient materials.

Many school districts provided these federally funded nursery schools. From 1933 to 1940, three hundred thousand children were enrolled in these schools, and in 1940 fifteen hundred such schools existed.[27] While studies showed that there were fewer teacher contacts with children, more verbal commands by teachers, a higher occurrence of petting and fondling of children, and more frequent use of deprivation and punishment in WPA schools as compared to university-centered schools,[28] in most cases the WPA schools offered a limited but still valuable educational experience to children.

---

[25]National Association for Nursery Education, National Committee on Nursery Schools, *Minimum Essentials for Nursery School Education* (Chicago: National Committee on Nursery Schools, 1929), 1.

[26]Catherine Landreth, *Education of the Young Child* (New York: John Wiley, 1942), 10.

[27]Ibid., 11.

[28]Catherine Landreth et al., "Teacher-Child Contacts in Nursery Schools," *Journal of Experimental Education* 12 (1943): 65–91.

World War II brought an end to the WPA programs as the unemployed teachers, nurses, nutritionists, cooks, and janitors found jobs. However, as women, including mothers of young children, were hired for war work, institutions were needed to care for their children. In 1941 Congress passed the Community Facilities Act, later called the Lanham Act, which established child care centers in "war-impacted" areas. Government support stopped after the war ended, and most of the centers closed.

A few of the Lanham Act schools continued to operate under local governmental support or philanthropic sponsorship. However, it should be recognized that the centers established under the Lanham Act were primarily for custodial care and not for nursery education. Indeed, some of these centers were kept open 24 hours a day to accommodate the women working different shifts at plants and factories.

The Lanham Act brought into focus the differences between the nursery school as an educational institution and the child care center as a custodial care institution for children of mothers who had to work because of economic necessity. The concept of "custodial care" was the core of the controversy that continued through the fifties and sixties between education-oriented program planners and welfare-oriented funding agencies. In addition, a heated argument against early childhood programs as "the enemy of family life" raged.[29]

Because of this controversy the growth of the nursery school movement slowed down until the 1960s. The one exception was the expanding number of parent-cooperative nursery schools. Many mothers were at home after the war and they wanted high quality nursery education at a reasonable cost. This was also the time when the field of child development and child rearing grew at a tremendous rate. Many mothers found the cooperative nursery school with its parent meetings a helpful vehicle for learning more about child development and rearing.

[29]Barbara Biber, *Early Education and Psychological Development* (New Haven, Conn.: Yale University Press, 1984), 9–26.

Head Start Programs

During the mid-1960s, the federal government again became involved in providing early childhood programs, this time for disadvantaged children. It came under the Economic Opportunity Act and the Elementary and Secondary Education Act which launched Head Start in 1965. The focus of the programs was to provide an environment in the preschool years that would, it was hoped, counteract the developmental disadvantages of growing up in poverty.

It is interesting to note that early Head Start programs were parallels of the McMillans' nursery school program in England; they were designed to be much more than a narrowly defined educational program. As it was originally conceived, Head Start included medical, dental, and social services. Nutrition and hygiene were as much a part of the program as education.

There is, however, a significant difference between the philosophies supporting each of these programs. As already mentioned, the nursery school movement in the beginning of this century used the metaphor of the garden to illustrate that education for the young child should follow the nature of the child, but not mold or impose upon it. While one could nurture and support the unfolding process, one could not greatly alter it. It was a generally held belief at this time that only frustration would result from pushing a child beyond his or her innate capability.

Around the 1960s a different, more egalitarian view of development emerged. This view was that under the right conditions all children, including the poor and especially the minority poor, could join in the mainstream of an affluent society if they were given a program of compensatory education. It was believed that development occurred through an interaction of the child with his or her environment. This interacting approach conceived of education as stimulating rather than merely supporting development.

This view of development was supported, and perhaps even caused, by two works published in the early 1960s. In the classic *Intelligence and Experience*[30] J. McVicker Hunt brought together data from many sources, including the work of the Swiss psychologist Jean Piaget, supporting the notion that experiences, especially those during the early childhood period, had a major impact on the developing intellect. Based on his analysis Hunt suggested that intelligence is not predetermined genetically at birth but instead it results to a great degree from the environmental encounters afforded the child. The other important work is the often cited study by Ben Bloom reported in *Stability and Change in Human Characteristics*.[31] Based on his analysis of test data on intelligence, he suggested that fifty percent of the variance in later intelligence tests could be accounted for by the variance in tests before the age of five. (It must be noted that Bloom's conclusion led to much confusion in early childhood education when the study was released and for some time afterwards. Some educators misinterpreted it to mean that 50 percent of a person's adult intelligence developed by age five and they pushed to introduce and force reading, writing, and math into preschools.)

Head Start represented a drastic change in the perceptions of Americans about the care needed for preschoolers and the relation of school to family and community. One of the dramatic changes called for teacher competence which lead to specially planned teacher-training programs and credentialing as a child development associate. By 1983, there were 10,000 credentialed associates[32], many of whom were working in the 1,800 Head Start programs throughout the country.

---

[30]J. McVicker Hunt, *Intelligence and Experience* (New York: Ronald, 1961).

[31]Benjamin S. Bloom, *Stability and Change in Human Characteristics* (New York: John Wiley, 1964).

[32]Barbara Biber, *Early Education and Psychological Development* (New Haven, Conn.: Yale University Press, 1984), 28.

The impact and effectiveness of Head Start have been controversial topics from the beginning. Hundreds of studies have been conducted producing widely varying results of the project's effectiveness. One recent government-sponsored report, *The Impact of Head Start on Children, Families and Communities,* came about as a result of a "meta-analysis" of available studies of Head Start's impact. This hefty document which includes a bibliography of more than 1,600 reports about Head Start was sent to Congress in August 1985, and the general findings of the meta-analysis are as follows:

> Children enrolled in Head Start enjoy significant imme-
> diate gains in cognitive test scores, socioemotional
> test scores and health status. In the long run, cognitive
> and socioemotional test scores of former Head Start
> students do not remain superior to those of disadvan-
> taged children who did not attend Head Start. However,
> a small subset of studies finds that former Head Starters
> are more likely to be promoted to the next grade and are
> less likely to be assigned to special education classes.
> Head Start also has aided families by providing health,
> social and educational services and by linking families
> with services available in the community. Finally, edu-
> cational, economic, health care, social service and other
> institutions have been influenced by Head Start staff and
> parents to provide benefits to both Head Start and non-
> Head Start families in their respective communities.[33]

True to form, soon after the 1985 report was published articles appeared in the literature questioning the value of the results of the meta-analysis on several grounds. For example, criticism was leveled at the fact that the studies included were not based on a representative sample of national Head Start sites, that many poorly designed studies were included, that some findings were based on very few studies that were designed for other

---

[33]R.H. McKey et al., *The Impact of Head Start on Children, Families and Communities,* Final Report of the Head Start Evaluation, Synthesis and Utilization Project (Washington, D.C.: CSR, Inc., June 1985), 1.

purposes, that conclusions about long-term efficacy should have been based on additional longitudinal studies, etc.[34] Regardless of these criticisms, there is a consensus in the literature agreeing with the authors of the report who maintain that, given what is known about preschool programs for children at risk of school failure, a renewed commitment to Head Start and its improvement is needed.

Child Care Centers

Child care centers, which were formerly called day nurseries and are today also called day care centers, comprise a diverse variety of establishments for the care of children whose parents cannot be at home when needed or cannot adequately provide for the needs of their children. There is family day care, where a caregiver provides services in his or her own home to a limited number of children; public child care centers financed by federal, state, or local funds; proprietary child care centers operated as businesses for profit; and nonprofit centers underwritten by industries or operated by churches and other community groups, often with flexible tuitions, to mention just a few types. In addition to caring for preschoolers, many of these establishments care for nursery school and school-age children before and after school and during vacations.

The spread of child care centers is a product of the Industrial Revolution. With the rise of the factory system and the hiring of large numbers of women and older children, a need appeared to care for young children who were separated from their mothers and older siblings during the day. These day nurseries, as they were called, served only the lower, working class who could not afford the servants that the middle and upper classes could.

The American day nursery was fashioned after the French *creche*, which was first established in Paris in 1844 to help working mothers. In the United States the New York Nursery and

---

[34]One of the most comprehensive articles is Lawrence Schweinhart and David Weikart, "What Do We Know so Far?: A Review of the Head Start Synthesis Project," *Young Children* 41 (January 1986): 49–55.

Child's Hospital in 1854 and the Philadelphia Day Nursery Association in 1863 opened child care facilities for working women.[35] At the New York Hospital, the day nursery was established in part to provide care for the children of wet nurses since these children often died for lack of sufficient milk.[36] The first federally funded day nurseries were established for a short time during the Civil War for war widows who needed care for their children so they could work.[37]

Industrialization, urbanization, and immigration caused day nurseries to abound during the last quarter of the nineteenth century. Many were established by settlement houses or under philanthropic auspices in order to help immigrants and poor working mothers, especially widows who otherwise would have had to abandon their children to residential institutions. Matrons, or nursery attendants, cleaned and prepared meals at day nurseries and were also responsible for keeping the children fed, clean, and safe.[38]

There was little if any educational program in day nurseries during this time. In fact, reports claim they were at best a custodial service, and at worst, dens for the neglect and abuse of children. Ethel Beer, for example, described the Brightside Nursery in New York City as it looked in 1915 as follows:

> A memorial window in the Nursery department effectively kept out the light, and row after row of ugly iron cribs ... left little space to play on the floor. Older preschool children did not even have cots for their rest period. Instead, they napped sitting up, their arms

[35]Ilse Forest, *Preschool Education: A Historical and Critical Study* (New York: Macmillan, 1927), 11.

[36]Margaret O'Brien Steinfels, *Who's Minding the Children?* (New York: Simon & Schuster, 1973), 36.

[37]National Society for the Study of Education, *Pre-School and Parental Education: Twenty-eighth Yearbook* (Bloomington, Ill.: Public School Publishing, 1929), 47.

[38]Lee C. Deighton, ed. *Encyclopedia of Education* (New York: Macmillan and the Free Press, 1971), s.v. "Day Care Centers," by Sadie D. Ginsberg.

cushioning their heads on the tables in front of them. Both boys and girls wore checked gingham pinafores over their own clothes, which were not always clean. Meals were served in shifts in the dining room, one group waiting in line for another to finish.

Zealous to relieve the plight of working mothers, it was often overcrowded. Regimentation was the rule rather than the exception.... The toys, frequently the discards of more fortunate boys and girls, were in the cupboards as much as in the children's hands. On the whole, the personnel was untrained and some were mentally dull. The diet was sadly lacking in vitamins. Orange juice and cod-liver oil were considered too extravagant to provide. Even milk was a scarce commodity, and the majority of children drank cocoa diluted with water.[39]

The nursery school movement in the 1920s introduced trained teachers into day nurseries. It is interesting to note that as day nurseries slowly began to take on an educative aspect, they began to exclude babies since teachers were not prepared to care for them. When the matrons and nursery attendants were replaced, very young children were barred from the day nursery, and ultimately the admission of toddlers too was restricted.

Around this same period, the professional social worker emerged and took great interest in day nurseries. Their predecessors, the early charity workers, believed that the day nursery was a service to mothers who had to work. The modern social worker saw it instead as a social welfare agency. Margaret O'Brien Steinfels maintains that the advent of the "high-minded" social worker after World War I marked the beginning of a long process of change in day care in this country from a useful, broadly defined, simple child-helping service to a marginal and limited agency of social welfare. She further believes that, except

---

[39]Ethel S. Beer, *Working Mothers and the Day Nursery* (New York: Whiteside, 1957), 43–44; quoted in Margaret O'Brien Steinfels, *Who's Minding the Children?* (New York: Simon & Schuster, 1973), 48–49.

for a brief interlude during World War II, the expansion and contraction of child care services occurred "without particular reference to the needs of working mothers."[40]

The Lanham Act of 1941 provided 50% of the funds for the care of children whose mothers were engaged in war industries. After the war, funding was terminated, and the generally accepted attitude that child care was child welfare resurfaced along with the attached stigma. Therefore, child care centers diminished in numbers and in visibility.

During the past two decades the demand for quality child care has grown. As more middle class and divorced women sought jobs, child care centers appeared to meet their demands. A change in attitude toward child care centers also occurred as a result of such factors as the changing status of women, further increase in urbanization, and a shift to a nuclear family. At the same time the stigma lessened as studies acknowledged that good quality child care did not have a negative effect on the young child, and that daily separation of mother from child during working hours was not comparable to total separation.

With the increase in demand for child care programs by working mothers, the sponsorship of these programs changed. The majority of facilities prior to the 1970s were sponsored by community, church, and philanthropic agencies with a few for-profit centers. Today, a majority of centers operate for profit, and franchises and chains abound. Centers that accept infants as young as six weeks are not uncommon.

It should be noted that for-profit centers do not necessarily provide good quality care. Even though all states have licensing standards for minimum acceptable levels for child care, the standards of quality are low. This is due to the nature of regulatory powers and to pressures to maintain low standards. Most licensing standards are confined to the material conditions of facilities, such as the number of sinks and toilets, lack of

[40]Margaret O'Brien Steinfels, *Who's Minding the Children?* (New York: Simon & Schuster, 1973), 57–63.

peeling paint, and the ratio of workers to children. The training
of personnel and the provision of educational programs usually
fall outside the purview of the licensing agencies.

Over the years there have been numerous studies to
determine if there are negative effects on children in child care
compared to children cared for at home, and other studies to
identify the positive elements in child care programs. In 1982
Bettye Caldwell and Marjorie Freyer reviewed this data and
concluded that a few research-based inferences can be drawn for
child care programs: (1) the programs should be kept small; (2)
attachment of children to their parents is not impaired by early
childhood care; (3) staff turnover may be less harmful than had
been feared; (4) the health of infants in groups can apparently be
maintained; (5) there is a need to re-evaluate the practice of
setting limits on children (studies suggested that children
showed superior language development in family day care
where, like at their own homes, they are exposed to more
prohibitions and corrections and restraints than children in
group child care); (6) the studies offer little curriculum guidance
in the different kinds of daily programs; and (7) parent
involvement takes many forms and remains elusive and difficult
to attain for many child care programs.[41]

While positive effects have been shown for high quality
child care programs, the availability of these programs remains
very limited. Furthermore, quality programs for preschoolers
are expensive when they can be found. Good teachers and
caregivers demand higher salaries. If one considers the results
from Caldwell and Freyer's research, programs should remain
small and child-staff ratios low. As long as preschool child care
depends on tuition alone, quality programs will remain hard to
find in many communities. The issue of federal support for
preschool programs continues to be raised, but it is still not
certain that such support will be provided in the near future.

---

[41]Bettye M. Caldwell and Marjorie Freyer, "Day Care and Early
Education," in *Handbook of Research in Early Childhood Education*, ed.
Bernard Spodek (New York: Free Press, 1982), 367–8.

Rationale for Sharing Books with Preschoolers

IN A SPEECH presented at an early childhood conference for librarians, Dorothy Butler eloquently states the value of sharing books with young children:

> Babies and small children need precision, beauty, lilt and rhythm, and the opportunity to look and to listen, as well as to touch and feel and smell. Words are finely tuned instruments which must be encountered early if their shades of meaning are to serve the developing intellect and emotions. There must be a two-way flow. There is no substitute for the loving exchange between adult and [young child], each determined to communicate by whatever method springs to mind and hand. Lifelong habits are entrenched in this apparently simple exchange.[1]

Even though librarians and many parents have long realized the value of introducing young children to books, the rationale for doing so has recently received renewed support from the work of early childhood educators. Within the past five years, the concept of "emergent literacy"[2] has become popular in the field

---

[1]Dorothy Butler, "Saying It Louder," *School Library Journal* 35 (September 1989): 156–57.

[2]In her 1966 doctoral dissertation, "Emergent Reading Behaviour," (University of Auckland, New Zealand) Marie Clay used this term.

of early childhood education. At the core of emergent literacy is the belief that "literacy development," or reading and writing behaviors and attitudes, begins long before the child starts formal instruction. The concept of emergent literacy maintains that children learn written language by interacting with parents and other adults in both reading and writing experiences, by exploring print on their own, and by watching how the adults around them read and write.

Emergent literacy is replacing reading readiness as the core concept of literacy development in children. Reading readiness was believed by two different schools of thought to come about either as the result of neural ripening or as a product of environmental experiences. In an essay about the history of reading development, Teale and Sulzby claim that the idea of reading readiness, which was strongly supported from the 1920s until very recently by preprimary and elementary schools and publishers of "pre-reading" materials, affected the public's thinking about literacy development in two ways. First, it led the public to believe that what happened during the preschool years was only the precursor to "real" reading, implying that the young child had to first master subskills before the reading process could begin. Second, and more importantly, it told the public that learning to read and write began in schools where the "readiness" skills could be properly taught.[3]

The concept of emergent literacy has led librarians and other educators to be even more aware of the important role parents play when they introduce the riches of books and literature-centered activities to young children in a natural way. Aidan Chambers reflects the beliefs of many when he said: "We have to acknowledge that the best and most lasting success comes only when the home environment is right-minded.... We have,

---

While not necessarily the originator of the term emergent literacy, Clay is credited with bringing the concept to the forefront.

[3]William H. Teale and Elizabeth Sulzby, "Emergent Literacy as a Perspective for Examining How Young Children Become Writers and Readers," in *Emergent Literacy: Writing and Reading,* edited by Teale and Sulzby (Norwood, N.J.: Ablex, 1986).

in fact, at last begun to recognize that any child who comes to school at five without certain kinds of literary experiences is a deprived child in whose growth there are deficiencies already too difficult to make good."[4]

Why Book Experiences?

The rationale for sharing books with preschoolers has been stated in various ways over many years. The following reasons why preschoolers are believed to benefit from books embody research findings as well as conventional wisdom:

Book experiences establish so called "literacy development," or reading and writing behaviors and attitudes.

There is a growing literature about children who read early. During the past 25 years, research has been conducted to determine what variables influence reading, and studies have concluded that children who read naturally either before formal schooling or soon thereafter were those who as young children had had extensive story-reading experiences.[5] In *Family Literacy*, Denny Taylor states that for the parents and children participating in her research, "reading and writing are cultural activities intrinsic to their experiences.... They join with speaking and listening in an elaboration of the families' existing association."[6]

It is interesting to note that two of the major studies concerning children who began to read before school, one by

---

[4]Aidan Chambers, *Introducing Books to Children* (Portsmouth, N.H.: Heinemann, 1973), 3.

[5]M.H. Sutton, "Readiness for Reading at the Kindergarten Level," *The Reading Teacher* 17 (1964): 234–40; Margaret M. Clark, *Young Fluent Readers: What They Can Teach Us* (London: Heinemann, 1976); Dolores Durkin, *Children Who Read Early: Two Longitudinal Studies* (New York: Teachers College Press, 1966); David Doake, "Book Experience and Emergent Reading in Preschool Children," (Ph.D. diss., University of Alberta, Edmonton, 1981); and Gordon Wells, *Learning through Interaction: The Study of Language Development* (Cambridge, Eng.: Cambridge University Press, 1981).

[6]Denny Taylor, *Family Literacy: Young Children Learning to Read and Write* (Exeter, N.H.: Heinemann, 1983), 80.

Dolores Durkin working with children in California and New York, and the other by Margaret Clark working with children in Glasgow, Scotland, had very similar findings. Few of the children had been a part of any kind of direct teaching of reading. Instead, parents or siblings answered the children's questions, such as the request for a pronunciation or a meaning of a word, and then left the children to continue their task alone. Most of the children engaged in active writing as they learned to read, and most children showed a great interest in print in their environment, such as on labels or the names of cars. Clark also reported on the importance of the local library in the experience of the early readers she studied.[7]

The numerous studies on early readers include children who came from different economic classes, had parents with various levels of formal schooling, had different numbers of siblings at home, etc. Early readers displayed few similar characteristics with the exception of one common variable in their backgrounds: book experiences.

Preschoolers who have a background of repeated experiences with books develop certain attitudes and knowledge. These children will have acquired:

- A taste for books. Don Holdaway in *The Foundations of Literacy* claims that such children have developed certain expectations of print and that this serves as a motivational factor. "They come to print with expectations, not only that they will succeed in unlocking its mysteries, but also that the mysteries are *worth* unlocking." They appreciate the special rewards of print and seek out book experiences. They are also curious about other aspects of print such as signs, labels, and advertisements. [8]

---

[7]Margaret M. Clark, *Young Fluent Readers: What They Can Teach Us* (London: Heinemann, 1976), and Dolores Durkin, *Children Who Read Early: Two Longitudinal Studies* (New York: Teachers College Press, 1966).

[8]Don Holdaway, *The Foundations of Literacy* (Portsmouth, N.H.: Heinemann, 1979), 49–62.

- A knowledge of some basic conventions about books. For example, one must know that books have a front and a back, that they begin and end in certain places, that pages turn from right to left and that books are read from front to back, left to right and top to bottom.[9]

- A knowledge of some basic conventions about print. Educators claim that one of the fundamental insights children need if they are to learn to read is that print must make sense. Children understand that words are placed together in a purposeful manner so that the message unfolds from the print itself and not, for example, from the pictures.

  In *More Than the ABCs*, Judith Schickedanz asks the question about how children learn to expect that print should make sense. She maintains that one source is the experiences that reading picture books bring, since "the first and most abiding focus is on the meaning." When a child is read to, his or her attention is not directed toward particular letters or words but is rather on what the story is about. From the start, such experiences communicate the expectation that print needs to make sense.[10]

- Some understanding of the relationship between print and speech. A picture book with text helps develop this understanding in children because it allows them to see print in relation to the speech that it generates. The text in a preschooler's favorite picture books is familiar to the child: it is most often simple and predictable, and after repeated readings, the child may recite the text verbatim without actually knowing how to read words. According to Schickedanz, "this oral knowledge of the text provides a powerful monitoring device when children become

---

[9]Various languages, such as Hebrew, Japanese, and Chinese, have conventions that are different from books printed in English. Children would acquire the conventions of the books in their culture.

[10]Judith A. Schickedanz, *More Than the ABCs: The Early Stages of Reading and Writing* (Washington, D.C.: National Association for the Education of Young Children, 1986), 42.

interested in figuring out how the print they see on each page actually 'works' to represent the story they know how to say."[11]

In the beginning stage, children may think that each letter in a word represents a spoken syllable or word. They eventually see that this representation leaves them with too much print. They realize that print and speech need to relate differently than first thought, and they try another approach. Children experiment with various strategies until they discover the relationship between print and speech.

- An understanding that book language differs from conversational language. As Don Holdaway puts it, "spoken language is ... a kind of composite message coming from language in association with sensory context. In consequence, spoken language structures may be incomplete or ambiguous in themselves without being confusing, because the situation adds its own components to the meaning." In contrast, written language must carry full meaning. "It is more formal, more complete, and more textured than spoken language, and to avoid ambiguity it has distinctive structures which do not appear in spoken dialects."[12]

- A "sense of story." Such children have listened usually for extended periods of time to continuous book language that usually contains plot, dialog, and sequence. They are developing the strategies for understanding the structure of a story. For example, the children are developing the ability to follow a plot and sequences so that they are able to anticipate what might happen next, and the ability to create imaginary mental images.

---

[11]Ibid., 44.

[12]Don Holdaway, *The Foundations of Literacy* (Portsmouth, N.H.: Heinemann, 1979), 54.

Book experiences are an effective way to create "habits of mind," which Dorothy Butler describes as "the flavor or bent of an individual's habitual thought processes."[13]

Some say that the narrative is the most effective form of ordering our thinking[14] and that book experiences can bring order to our thinking by reinforcing the narrative.[15] Furthermore, Butler believes that such experiences are not only effective but are *simple*. She says: "Great changes are thought to require complex technology and huge sums of money. The simple triangle of parent, child, and book is not easily accepted as the passport it actually is to the essential qualities of life: The human capacities to love, laugh, and to learn."[16]

Books may help meet some basic needs of preschoolers.

In *The Years Before School*, Todd and Heffernan list the needs of the preschool child:

- The need for a secure, loving, and dependable relationship first with parents and then with other family members.

- The need to realize one's own worth.

- The need for adequate achievement.

- The need to belong to a group.

- The need for freedom from fear, or anxiety, or guilt.

- The need for a variety of experiences in one's world.[17]

Book experiences may contribute to meeting each one of these. There are many books that further a child's sense of

---

[13]Dorothy Butler, "Saying It Louder," *School Library Journal* 35 (September 1989): 156.

[14]Susanne K. Langer, *Feeling and Form* (New York: Scribner, 1953).

[15]Barbara Hardy, "Narrative as a Primary Act of the Mind," in *The Cool Web: The Pattern of Children's Reading*, ed. Margaret Meek, Aidan Warlow, and Griselda Barton (New York: Atheneum, 1978).

[16]Dorothy Butler, "Saying It Louder," *School Library Journal* 35 (September 1989): 159.

[17]Vivian Edmiston Todd and Helen Heffernan, *The Years Before School: Guiding Preschool Children*, 3rd ed. (New York: Macmillan, 1977), 446.

security within his family by portraying relationships between family members. Additionally, the mere act of sharing a book together usually provides the child with a sense of security.

There are books that help young children appreciate their own worth and build self-confidence. Stories that have a main character who overcomes difficulty and gains recognition help preschoolers in meeting the need for achievement. Young children who follow Harold on his adventures with his purple crayon can identify with him and enjoy Harold's achievements as he overcomes difficulties. Many books are available which show for them how to deal with the fears and anxieties of situations, such as the introduction of a new baby into the family, moving to a new house, or going to sleep.

There are many excellent books which help children gain a sense of belonging to a group, which for preschoolers means their families and a wider community, such as a preschool group. For example, stories that guide preschoolers through a first day at preschool can serve as a means for putting their experiences into perspective. Through stories, children reach an understanding of their world. They can enjoy descriptions of occurrences that are beyond their experiences. For example, preschoolers vicariously experience the sensations Peter Rabbit has when he is in the watering can in the shed, the feeling of security the little girl has when she outsmarts the gunnywolf, or the surprise Peter experiences when he discovers that the snow ball he put in his snowsuit pocket has melted after he has come indoors.

Book experiences provide pleasure for both the child and adult.

Holdaway claims that parents who read to their pre-schoolers do not engage in it as a duty or to achieve specific education advantages for the child.

It is a simple giving and taking of pleasure in which the parent makes no demands that normally arise. It provides a stimulus for satisfying interaction between parent and child, different, richer and more wide-ranging than the mundane interactions of running the home. *The major purpose from the parent's point of view is to give pleasure, and the parent is sustained in this behaviour by the ample bonuses provided.*[18]

On the other hand, the situation may be among some of the happiest and most secure in the child's life. The books themselves, if carefully selected, are satisfying. As Holdaway so eloquently says:

It provides an expansion of mental room, and freedom within it. The nature of the relationship with the parent is very special to the situation: the parent is giving complete attention; there are none of the normal distractions most of the time; the parent is invariably positive and interesting, with an enhanced being from association with the richness of the literature; and there is a feeling of security and special worth arising from the quality of the attention being received. *Thus the child develops strong positive associations with the flow of story language and with the physical characteristics of the books.*[19]

---

[18]Don Holdaway, *The Foundations of Literacy* (Portsmouth, N.H.: Heinemann, 1979), 39.

[19]Ibid., 40.

4

Developing the Schema

IT is hoped that this book will encourage librarians to develop, if they are not already doing so, literature-centered programs for preschoolers. Programs can be provided directly to the children by librarians or by parents, teachers, and caregivers. In the later case, it is hoped that this books will encourage librarians to develop literature-centered programs for the parents, teachers, and caregivers of preschoolers. However, before a librarian can develop either direct or indirect literature-centered programs appropriate for preschoolers, he or she must have some basic understanding of how preschoolers think and act.

In the following chapter, a "schema"[1] attempts to do this. In a broad sense, schema is defined as an outline. This particular one includes the salient characteristics of three- and four-year-olds. It also includes sets of suggestions that are derived from the characteristics for what librarians should be doing in story-times and in programs for parents and other adults who care for preschoolers.

The first step in developing the schema was to consult a large body of work in the field of child development. Numerous

---

[1]The term "schema" was originally used to define the chart of "growth characteristics with literature sharing implications for libraries" developed for my doctoral research dealing with library programs for children under three years of age. I have no fond attachment to the term schema, but continue to use the term for the sake of continuity between my previous book and this one.

resources, some general and some specific, were reviewed to develop the schema. Several child development texts[2] served as starting points.

Most general texts take an eclectic approach to describe child development. Instead of focusing on one particular theory of development, they incorporate the methods, ideas, and research findings from a spectrum of theoretical positions. Just as one may put "more stock" in one theory over another, so may an author of a general text. Therefore, the works of specific theorists were read in their original form.

The cognitive theory of Jean Piaget (1896–1980), the psychosocial or emotional theory of Erik Erikson (born 1902), and the maturational theory of Arnold Gesell (1880–1961) and his colleagues played important roles in developing the schema of this book. The depth and breadth of the work of these three figures have had a lasting influence in the field of early childhood development. A brief description of each is now provided.

Jean Piaget's Work in Cognition

Since the 1960s it has become increasingly evident to educators and child psychologists that Piaget is the most important contributor to the field of intellectual development. Starting in the 1920s, Piaget developed a theory which he promoted in his more than forty books and one hundred articles in child psychology.

In the 1920s, when much of the general public still regarded a child as a miniature adult, Piaget pointed out that the way a child's mind works is quite different from an adult's. A child perceives the world from a limited perspective which widens as he or she gets older and comes to think in the logical fashion we adults take for granted. Piaget also argued that the child is not a

---

[2]Sandra Anselmo, *Early Childhood Development: Prenatal through Age Eight* (Columbus, Ohio: Merrill, 1987); L.J. Stone and J. Church, *Childhood and Adolescence*, 4th ed. (New York: Random House, 1979); and Greta G. Fein, *Child Development* (Englewood Cliffs, N.J.: Prentice-Hall, 1978).

passive organism but rather an active participant in one's own development through interactions with the environment.

From his observations of children, especially his own three children, Piaget developed the theory that intellectual development takes place in stages through which every child passes in the same orderly progression. He maintained further that at each stage it is necessary for the environment to supply encounters for the child which permit him or her to use existing intelligence (assimilation) while, at the same time, forcing the child to modify her or his ideas (accommodation) if intellectual development is to progress.

Piaget was a precocious child who published his first scientific article when he was ten years old. He originally trained as a biologist and did his dissertation on mollusks, but he became interested in child psychology while working as a student in the laboratory of Alfred Binet (of the Stanford-Binet test fame) to refine items on the early Binet intelligence test.

During his interviews with children to refine the test, Piaget was intrigued by the "wrong" answers of children. He came to realize that these incorrect answers were part of the developmental process, leading eventually to the "right" answers of logical thought. He would set up a problem or an experiment and then ask the child what he or she thought would happen. The answers he received led him to believe that young children see the world and all of its occurrences in terms of their own experiences and emotional needs.

Piaget maintained that by the time most children are seven years old, they can distinguish two types of knowledge: that which is true most of the time and that which is necessarily true by deduction. Before this time, they can only consider the former type of knowledge. Piaget described the period from about age two to seven as the preoperational stage of intelligence. It is this period that we are most interested in for the purposes of this book.

During the preoperational stage, children's thinking is characterized by the development of language and symbolic imitation. For example, merely wearing a fire helmet can make children think they are being fire fighters. Play, which is largely symbolic imitation, occupies most of children's waking hours and is vital to this stage. As Piaget said, "One of the functions of symbolic play is to satisfy the self by transforming what is real into what is desired."

Another major developmental characteristic of this stage is egocentric thinking. Egocentricism does not refer to selfishness or arrogance in this context. Piaget argued that because children view the world from their own perspectives, it is difficult for them to imagine how an object or scene might look when viewed from positions other than their own. He also maintained that egocentricism can lead to misinterpretations of natural phenomena. For example, when he asked preschoolers why a marble rolled down a slope he was told "because it knows we're waiting for it," and when he asked about the moon he was told that it follows children "to watch over them." Moreover, during this period, egocentricism causes children to take it for granted that everyone thinks as they do and understands them. It is difficult for a preschooler who likes trucks to believe that his or her mother would not want a truck more than anything else as a gift. Here is how J.H. Flavell describes this stage:

> The preoperational child is the child of wonder; his cognition appears to us naive, impression-bound, and poorly organized. There is an essential lawlessness about his world without, of course, this fact in any way entering his awareness to inhibit the zest and flights of fancy with which he approaches new situations. Anything is possible because nothing is subject to lawful constraints.[3]

---

[3]J.H. Flavell, *The Developmental Psychology of Jean Piaget* (New York: Van Nostrand Reinhold, 1963), p.211.

It must be remembered that preoperational children's inability to think logically in adult terms does not necessarily mean that they are deficient thinkers. They are busy exploring, manipulating, questioning, comparing, contrasting, labelling and forming mental images, which are the foundation for the development of the ability to think logically. For Piaget, development was not a case of simply accumulating more data; in fact, he saw it as a case of having to remember less as the child developed the ability to make inferences logically.

In developing the schema, two of Piaget's works, *The Psychology of the Child*, which is an excellent summary of his theories, and *Play, Dreams, and Imitation in Childhood*, which describes the preoperational period of development, were the primary sources used to compile the sections on intellectual development. His other works relevant to preschool development[4] were also consulted.

Erik Erikson's Work in Psychosocial Development

As a young teacher in Vienna, Erik Erikson studied under Anna Freud, who trained him in child psychoanalysis. It was also during this period from 1927 to 1933 that Erikson obtained the only formal academic certificate he would receive, that as a Montessori teacher. However, in 1933 fascism in Europe prompted Erikson and his family to move to the United States, where he worked as a child analyst at Harvard and Yale.

Until 1939, he was known as Erik Homburger; however, when he faced a "rebirth" as an American citizen, he chose to be known as Erikson, the last name of his natural father who had abandoned his mother before his birth. During the following

---

[4]J. Piaget and B. Inhelder, *The Psychology of the Child* (New York: Basic Books, 1969); J. Piaget, *Play, Dreams, and Imitation in Childhood* (New York: Norton, 1951); J. Piaget and B. Inhelder, *The Child's Conception of Space* (London: Routledge and Kegan Paul, 1956); J. Piaget, B. Inhelder, and A. Szeminska, *The Child's Conception of Geometry* (New York: Basic Books, 1960); J. Piaget, *The Child's Conception of Time* (New York: Ballantine, 1969), J. Piaget, *The Language and Thought of the Child* (New York: Meridian, 1955).

dozen years he lived on the West Coast, where he studied children and conducted anthropological inquiries into child rearing practices among various groups including Native Americans.

Erikson is best known for the theoretical framework he presented in his first book, *Childhood and Society*:[5] that development is a synthesis of childhood and expected social tasks. In this work he states that psychosocial development is the basis of human development and he sets forth his "eight stages of man."

Very briefly, he maintains that infancy is a time for developing a sense of trust which lays the groundwork for a feeling of security throughout a person's life. During the two-year-old period, a sense of autonomy must be developed if the toddler is to move from dependence to independence and to experience the power of mastery which comes with walking, holding, and reaching. The third stage, when the child acquires a sense of initiative is the most important stage for the purposes of this book. Therefore, information about the characteristics of this stage has been included in the schema.

Children enter the third stage roughly around thirty-six months, and, if a firm sense of trust has been established and if they have mastered some measure of control over themselves during the second stage, a sense of initiative permeates the rest their lives. They have mastered skills of reaching, taking, and holding and are now combining these capabilities in a complex manner, e.g., skipping while holding a ball. Their use of language has also improved and they ask questions through which they begin to understand themselves and their environment. Armed with locomotion and language, preschoolers are now able to expand their activities and imaginations. Some of the possibilities will undoubtedly frighten them.

---

[5]E. Erikson, *Childhood and Society*, 2d rev. ed. (New York: Norton, 1963).

Erikson, like Piaget, believed that play served a major role during this period. Solitary play is important since children need time by themselves for activities and daydreaming during which to play or dream out conflicts and resolutions. Cooperative play is important since the company of other children is required to play out individual and mutual crises. Play relationships serve as opportunities for solving previous difficulties or in anticipating new problems.

The Gesell Institute's Work in Maturation

For centuries philosophers such as Rousseau held that development unfolds according to a set schedule. However, Arnold Gesell and his colleagues at Yale are credited as being the first researchers to conduct extensive and detailed studies of babies and children with the aim of describing the ages and stages of typical growth.

Gesell was born in Alma, Wisconsin and attended Clark University where he earned his Ph.D. in 1906 and came under the influence of G. Stanley Hall, one of the earliest psychologists to study child development. After graduating, Gesell spent several years as a teacher and principal in public schools, as a settlement worker, and as a university professor. In 1911 he founded the Clinic of Child Development at Yale. Even though he had been working as a successful psychologist and had gained substantial professional status, he decided that medicine would give him greater depth as a researcher. Accordingly, he studied medicine at Yale while he was an assistant professor and received his M.D. degree in 1915.

In his 50 years at the Yale Clinic, he and his researchers developed behavior norms which were so complete that they still serve as a source of information for pediatricians and psychologists today. Gesell also developed one of the first tests of infant intelligence and was among the first researchers to make extensive use of film observations of children.

Gesell's work centered on maturation, a general term he gave to the mechanism by which genes direct the development process. He looked at this process, which is distinct from the role of the environment, in both prenatal and postnatal development. His studies with identical twins conducted in the 1920s demonstrated that even though the twin who was given practice at such activities as stair-climbing and vocabulary showed some skill superior to that of the other, the untrained twin soon caught up. Moreover, the untrained twin did so at about the age at which we would expect the child to perform the various tasks. Gesell argued that an inner timetable exists that determines the readiness to do things, and that the benefits of early training are temporary.[6]

This does not mean that Gesell considered the environment unimportant. He pointed out that both prenatal and postnatal development required certain environmental conditions. In the 1940s he published findings showing that children in institutions whose environment was extremely impoverished in stimulation and care did not develop well. He believed that a favorable environment was necessary to support growth.

Gesell was also the best-known "baby doctor" from the 1930s until Spock published his famous book in 1945. Gesell rejected popular notions of the time and advocated such things as feeding a baby on demand rather than by a predetermined schedule. More generally he suggested that parents suspend their ideas about what a child "ought" to be doing at a particular age and follow the child's signals and cues.

Infant and Child in the Culture of Today by Gesell and the late Frances Ilg first appeared in 1943 and was widely read by parents. After Gesell retired in 1950, his colleagues, including Frances Ilg, Louise Bates Ames, and Janet Rodell, founded the Gesell Institute of Child Development in his honor. Research and publications which support Gesell's basic philosophy—that instead of controlling and directing children, parents should take time to watch, enjoy, and appreciate their children as they do

---

[6]A. Gesell and H. Thompson, "Learning and Growth in Identical Infant Twins: An Experimental Study by the Method of Co-twin Control," *Genetic Psychology Monographs* 6 (1929): 1–124.

their own growing—still continue to be produced by the Institute. In developing the schema, four recent publications from the Gesell Institute were used.[7]

Additional Sources

As previously stated, a heavy emphasis was placed on Piaget's theories in the development of the schema. J. McVicker Hunt's classic, *Intelligence and Experience,* a work which, as the title implies, focuses on the role of experience in the development of intelligence, was consulted. Particular attention was given to Chapters 5 through 7 which set forth the main themes of Piaget's works and the principles deriving from them. In addition, two articles which apply Piaget's theory to preschool education were reviewed.[8]

Since language learning is one of the major developments of this period, sources dealing with language were included in the review. In learning language children do not merely imitate adult speech. Instead, they take the language they hear around them, filter it through their own minds, and then construct their own speech.

The two most useful works on this topic were Roger Brown's *A First Language: The Early Stages,* an account of three children and their early grammatical rule learning, and Peter A. and Jill

[7]A. Gesell, F. Ilg, and L.B. Ames, *Infant and Child in the Culture of Today: The Guidance of Development in Home and Nursery School,* rev. ed. (New York: Harper & Row, 1974); L.B. Ames et al., *The Gesell Institute's Child from One to Six: Evaluating the Behavior of the Preschool Child* (New York: Harper & Row, 1979); L.B. Ames and F. Ilg, *Your Three-Year-Old: Friend or Enemy* (New York: Delta, 1976); and L.B. Ames and F. Ilg, *Your Four-Year-Old: Wild and Wonderful* (New York: Delta, 1976).

[8]J. McVicker Hunt, *Intelligence and Experience* (New York: Ronald, 1961); Constance Kamii, "A Sketch of the Piaget-Derived Curriculum Developed by the Ypsilanti Early Education Program," in *History and Theory of Early Childhood Education,* ed. S.J. Braun and E. Edwards (Worthington, Ohio: Charles A. Jones, 1972); and George E. Forman and Catherine Ywomey Fosnot, "The Use of Piaget's Constructivism in Early Childhood Education Programs," in *Handbook of Research in Early Childhood Education,* ed. B. Spodek (New York: Free Press, 1982).

G. de Villiers's *Early Language*, a comprehensive summary of early language development from birth to age six. Lev Vygotsky's *Thought and Language* was also consulted, as was Kornei Chukovsky's *From Two to Five*, which describes the verbal creativity of the preschooler.[9]

Play is very hard work for the preschooler. It is the natural way for a child to learn and use skills, to explore, to concentrate, to imagine, and to test ideas. At the same time, it gives the child a feeling of power and offers relief from a sense of frustration and inadequacy. Moreover, play provides a base for language and facilitates building relationships with other children. The Singers at Yale University have conducted studies dealing with the preschooler and play. Two excellent titles by them in addition to other books dealing with the role that play plays in preschool development were consulted. [10]

To make certain that current important studies were included, several edited collections were reviewed.[11] These were very helpful in developing the schema.

Finally, dozens of popular titles intended for parents were reviewed.[12] By and large, the books intended for parents offered

[9]Roger Brown, *A First Language: The Early Stages* (Cambridge, Mass.: Harvard University Press, 1973); Peter A. and Jill G. de Villiers, *Early Language* (Cambridge, Mass.: Harvard University Press, 1979); Lev Vygotsky, *Thought and Language* (Cambridge, Mass.: MIT Press, 1962); and Kornei Chukovsky, *From Two to Five* (Berkeley: University of California Press, 1965).

[10]Jerome Singer, *The Child's World of Make Believe* (New York: Academic, 1977); Dorothy G. and Jerome Singer, *Partners in Play* (New York: Harper & Row, 1977); Catherine Garvey, *Play* (Cambridge, Mass.: Harvard University Press, 1977); and Frank and Theresa Caplan, *The Power of Play* (New York: Doubleday, 1973).

[11]Bernard Spodek, *Handbook of Research in Early Childhood Education* (New York: Free Press, 1982); S.G. Moore and C.R. Cooper, *The Young Child: Reviews of Research* (Washington, D.C.: NAEYC, 1982); Mollie and Russell Smart, *Preschool Children: Development and Relationships* (New York: Macmillan, 1973); and Greta Fein and M. Rivkin, *The Young Child at Play: Reviews of Research* (Washington, D.C.: NAEYC, 1986).

[12]For example, James Comer and Alvin Poussaint's *Black Child Care: How to Bring up a Healthy Black Child in America* (New York: Simon &

parenting tips and techniques, and therefore played hardly any role in the development of the schema.

Schuster, 1976), Joseph Sparling and Isabelle Lewis' *Learning Games for Threes and Fours: A Guide to Adult/Child Play* (New York: Walker, 1984), and Carol Tomlinson-Keasey's *Child's Eye View* (New York: St. Martin's, 1980), to name just a few, were read.

5

The Schema

AN IMPORTANT GOAL of library programs is to instill a love of books and reading early in life. Even though the development of language, listening and looking skills, and reinforcement of concepts are important immediate objectives of activities for preschoolers, they should never be emphasized to the point where the child's enjoyment of books is jeopardized. A caring adult who shares literature with a young child provides that child with a feeling of security and a time for enjoyment. These pleasurable experiences may not only make it easier for the child to learn to read when the time comes, but may also help develop a lifetime reading habit.

However, activities meant to foster the love of books, if they are to fulfill their purpose, must be developmentally appropriate for the children. Thus, what adults—librarians, parents, teachers, and caregivers—should be doing for preschoolers hinges directly on the nature of the children. This chapter presents a compilation of salient developmental characteristics of three- and four-year-old children followed by implications for library programs drawn from these characteristics.

Since many library programs are designed specifically for either three-years-olds or four-year-olds, this arbitrary but convenient division is employed below. It should be kept in mind, however, that human development is continuous and only loosely synchronized with chronological age, and that library programs should ideally be based on children's developmental levels. The listed characteristics are those of an "average" child; they will fit any particular child only approximately.

Three Years of Age: Developmental Characteristics

Language Development

- For children of this age, talking may be more important than listening.

- The child talks out loud about and describes what he or she is doing or plans to do; however, this does not necessarily mean that the three-year-old wants to communicate with others.[1]

- They enjoy talking for the fun of it and delight in language play, not requiring that every word carry meaning: some phrases have melody or humor, some are chants.

- They speak in short sentences and usually with animation.

- They use new words and plurals with ease. A child's vocabulary expands as he or she learns new concepts and the words which denote them. The average vocabulary sizes for three- and three-and-a-half-year-old children are 1,000 and 1,200 words, respectively.

- They recognize and name most parts of the body as well as familiar objects and pictures of them.

- They may use pronouns incorrectly and be confused by them. For example, when a mother says, "It is my birthday" the child may interpret it to mean it is his or her own birthday.

- They are able to recite the alphabet or numbers from 1 to 20. However, this does not reflect real understanding of the underlying concepts. Instead, the recitation is a series of verbalizations and may be associated with an activity, such

---

[1]The Russian psychologist Lev Vygotsky suggests that this type of speech helps the preschooler attach words to the actions of play.

as counting to ten in preparation for running or kicking a ball.

- At age three-and-a-half, even though they have better command of language than at three, "disequilibrium"[2] may produce stuttering and affect speech. Children's vocabulary, even though growing, cannot keep pace with their thoughts.

- The child speaks with other children in the sense that conversation slowly becomes reciprocal; he or she now talks with, not just to, other children.

- Their questioning is in earnest, and children will often ask why, how, what, when.

- By age three-and-a-half, most baby talk has been discarded even though some errors in pronunciations such as "dis" for "this" and "wide" for "ride" may remain.

- They do not understand idioms or other nonliteral uses of words. For example, children cannot comprehend that the statement "it is raining cats and dogs" has nothing to do with cats or dogs.

- In spite of their growing language ability, much of a three-year-old's communication with others is nonverbal.

Intellectual Development

- The child views the world egocentrically so that he or she has difficulty thinking from another's point of view.

- They have fixed perceptions. Children believe what they see and can focus usually on only one attribute of an object at a time. This is usually the predominant feature.[3]

- They are only at the threshold of abstraction. Children must first build a base of experiences and see relationships among them before they are able to form an abstraction.

---

[2]Gesell and Ames use this term to describe periods of tension and insecurity.

[3]Piaget terms this "centering" and argues that it prevents children from observing other properties of an object simultaneously.

- They are busy observing their world both firsthand and in pictures and getting names to go with the objects they see.

- They understand the concept of "time" in the dual sense of the present and the past by establishing two distinct and separate points in time, e.g., thinking of themselves as they are now and as they were in the past as infants.

- They are extremely curious about people, events, and things around them, and ask many questions.

- They have a keen interest in living and growing things, especially animals, and find them fascinating to watch.

- Their reasoning is powerful enough so that they may be able to predict what may happen next in a story or to understand simple trickery or humor.

- They enjoy listening to music and making music with their voices, hands, feet, and by hitting objects.

- When classifying objects, children find it easiest to work with gross categories such as big and small or tall and short, with little or no middle range within categories.

- As in the case of objects, when classifying sex roles, children find it easiest to do so based on gross differences. A child may initially imitate behavior that is clearly male or clearly female.

- They enjoy matching and naming activities, simple guessing and pretend games, and "what comes next?" activities.

Motor Development

- They have good balance and control in gross and fine motor behavior of hands, legs, and total body.

- They control speed of running and walking, can easily alternate feet when climbing stairs (but not necessarily when descending), and are able to stand on one foot momentarily or walk on tiptoe.

- They enjoy riding a tricycle; they catch a ball with arms straight.

- They enjoy galloping, jumping, walking, marching, and running to music with vigor, and are able to swing arms freely while doing so.

- They are able to undo buttons and zippers and may be more interested in getting undressed than dressed.

- They are interested in projects that require finer motor manipulation, such as drawing with crayons, markers, or pencils (they can copy a circle and reproduce a cross if shown how), playing with small blocks and cubes (they can build a tower of nine to ten cubes), or using scissors to cut paper.

- At age three-and-a-half, children may experience "disequilibrium" and be less secure and effective physically; they may stumble, tremble, and show fear of falling; they may experience eye blinking and poor visual coordination.

Emotional and Personality Development

- Children may consider it more important to get things started than to finish them. Planning and exploring are the essence of the preschool period.

- They show pride in being able to feed and partially dress themselves and in washing and drying their hands and faces.

- They are eager to be with other children or adults and are usually easy to get along with; they respond positively to encouragement, praise, and consistent direction.

- Their growing imagination may cause them to experience fantastic fears of dogs, water, going down drains in bathtubs and toilets, loud noises, or the dark.

- They enjoy repetition and choruses in stories, songs, poems, and finger plays since it provides them with a sense of achievement and an opportunity to participate in the activity.

- Children are egocentric and their thoughts are mostly about themselves and about the other members of their households; they are unable to understand people from households different from their own.

- They are interested in babyhood and especially in their own recent infancy.

- Children experience a close relationship with grandparents and usually enjoy being with them.

- "Disequilibrium" at three-and-a-half may cause bouts of emotional turmoil where there is little cooperation and much negative behavior which may directed only at principal caregiver, such as the mother. For example, nothing about a meal a mother makes is right: The type of food, its amount, the way it is put on the plate, or even the way a sandwich is cut.

- They may resort to thumb sucking, nail biting, nose picking, or hugging a security blanket during tense times or when they are weary, thwarted, or sick.

- They thrive in a structured environment and may be made uncomfortable by changes in daily routines. In their own way children are attempting to develop self-restraint and need structure to aid them.

- They are eager to help with actual chores, such as watering plants, wiping tables, and putting toys away.

- If a sibling is born, they may feel jealous and demand attention.

Social Development

- They discover that behavior acceptable within their own family may be very different from that accepted outside the family.

- It may be difficult for them to share or be generous since it often means giving up the object they are playing with or the

food they are eating. Children are more likely to be per-
suaded by the merits of a "trade."

- They understand taking turns and are starting to understand
the concept of cooperation (which is very different from the
concept of sharing).

- Although children are usually more cooperative than before
and want to please adults, they may revert to toddler
behavior (thumb sucking, crying, baby talk) when faced
with a new or unpleasant setting.

- They are able to cooperatively play with other children.
Parallel play, found in earlier stages, is gradually displaced
by more cooperation between children. A verbal give-and-
take emerges that indicates a limited but real awareness of
others.

- They enjoy all types of play. It serves as their main tool for
mastering the environment. Repetitious play is the key to
mastery, and they voluntarily repeat actions.

- They delight in playing with simple hand puppets either
alone or in a small group.

- They enjoy circle and simple movement games in a group,
such as "London Bridge," "Farmer in the Dell," and "Ring
around the Rosie."

- They play well in a small group with one or two other
children of both sexes, with blocks and toys, but may not be
ready for play groups with many children.

- "Disequilibrium" at three-and-a-half may cause bouts of
social turmoil so that cooperation is extremely difficult.
Children may express negative behavior towards their
principal caregiver, who is usually the mother, and are often
happier and better behaved with other caregivers.

Three Years of Age: Implications for Library Programs

Library programs for three-year-olds include both storytimes for the children and programs designed for parents and other adults who care for and teach children. Since many three-year-olds attend preschool, serious effort should be made to reach and introduce literature-centered informational programs to those adults who have lengthy contact with children in preschool.

Librarians planning *storytimes* for three-year-olds should find the following list of suggestions helpful:

- The library should be an inviting place for preschoolers to visit. It can be decorated with realistic pictures of people's faces, friendly animals, children and their families, and familiar objects hung at children's eye level; with child-sized furniture; and with other interesting displays.

- Since children of this age are active and may be more interested in starting than in finishing activities, intersperse the storytime with activities that involve the children, such as finger plays, creative dramatics, and sing-alongs. Keep the pace brisk but calm.

- For the child, talking may be more important than listening, so be patient but firm when a child interrupts. Inform the child that there will be time after the story when he or she can talk. Be certain to allow time later for the question or comment to be addressed.

- When several children in a group are eager to talk, help them learn how to take turns. First, point the problem out to make the children aware of it. ("When we all talk, we can't hear anyone.") Then, present the solution involving taking turns. ("We can take turns. Let's do it this way. When you have something to say, you raise your hand and I'll call on you when it's your turn.")

- Children often ask questions they already know the answer to with the hope that they will be asked by the adult to answer it themselves. Oblige the child; ask the preschooler if he or she has any ideas about what the answer may be.

- Unless you are certain that the story will be misunderstood without discussing the meaning of some word, wait until the story is completed before explaining the meaning of the word.

- If possible, allow children to engage in word play by repeating refrains in stories or poems as you read them. This practice can also build listening skills since children must listen and be ready when it is time to say the refrain. Some librarians find it helpful to use a hand signal which the children recognize as the cue. For example, a hand in the air above the book may be a sign for children to begin, and a hand lowered to the top of the book a sign to stop.

- In order to encourage children's language development, speak to them in a way which is easy to hear and imitate accurately. Speak distinctly, pleasantly, calmly, and with only a few well-chosen words at a time. Listen carefully to their responses. During conversations before and after library programs, face the child and give full attention to the conversation. Squatting or kneeling to the same level as the child helps both the adult and child to communicate.

- Be patient if a child stutters when responding to a question. Let the child complete his or her thought. Try not to correct grammar and to call attention to the child in front of others. The preschooler will gradually make his or her imperfect language more and more grammatically correct.

- If possible, help children understand how to interpret pictures they are looking at. Ask the children to discuss what is happening in the picture. For instance, a child may assume that a character has lost a part of his arm if it is not shown in the picture.

- Parents/teachers/caregivers should be provided with details about the stories and activities, such as booklists or printed handouts of finger plays and poems so that books and activities can be repeated with their children later. Do this either before or after the storytime.

In selecting stories and activities[4] for three-year-olds, librarians should choose:

- Stories and activities that have straightforward plots, large, clear illustrations, and brief text.

- Stories and activities with pictures realistic in their general outlines and free from confusing detail.

- Stories and activities that have at most a few main characters who are understandable, both in text and in illustration, to the children.

- Stories and activities with a great deal of repetition.

- Stories and activities about everyday, actual experiences. These have been referred to as "here and now" literature.

- Simple, descriptive stories and activities about community helpers which avoid sex stereotyping and which will help children form realistic concepts about different vocations.

- Simple, factually correct informational books that answer common questions that concern the three-year-old.

- Stories and activities which span a variety of language patterns among them. Children need to hear varied uses of language if they are to understand and use more complex language. Librarians should become aware of the different kinds of language used in different books since authors vary widely in their use of English.

---

[4]Activities is used here as a catchall term to refer to related activities that librarians have traditionally included in preschool storytimes. These include: (1) conducting finger plays and simple creative dramatics; (2) telling stories using flannel boards, chalk boards, or magnetic boards; (3) showing large pictures, study prints, or realia for the children to look at while, for instance, a poem is being recited; and (4) showing short films, videos, or filmstrips based on children's literature. Individual library settings will determine what type of activities are used.

- Mother Goose verses, which contain superb rhythm, rhyme, language patterns, and word play. Many three-year-olds have heard Mother Goose verses at home, so that hearing them provides a link between home and the library and fosters a feeling of security.

- Stories and activities that include a few unfamiliar words. Children even as young as three can often determine the meaning of words if they are presented in context. If there are words that are unfamiliar enough to the children to need explaining, the book is probably too difficult and should be used with an older group.

- Stories and activities based on real people, animals, and events but containing the imaginative, such as Esphyr Slobodkina's *Caps for Sale*. These have been referred to as transitional literature since they bridge the stage between the experiential "here and now" story and the truly imaginative story. These stories seem to be based in reality until they introduce something just over the border into the imaginary, separating the real from the impossible.

- Stories and activities that include simple guessing, pretending, matching and naming, and anticipating what comes next.

- Musical activities that include marching, singing, and clapping during the storytime.

- Circle and simple movement games such as "Farmer in the Dell," "London Bridge," and "Ring around the Rosie."

- Before or after the storytimes, songs from recordings for children by, among others, Hap Palmer, Ella Jenkins, Woody Guthrie, Rafi, or Tom Glazer.

- Stories and activities that stimulate the children's interest and also foster feelings of self-confidence, security, and the need for cooperation.

- Stories and activities about topics that interest three-year-olds.[5] Using a topic or theme provides a thread that can serve as a reinforcement of vocabulary and concepts. However, a topic needs to make sense to the three-year-old and should not be forced by the librarian. For example, using a topic of rabbits and including Margaret Wise Brown's *The Runaway Bunny* is inappropriate since the book is not about rabbits. It is true that the mother and child are rabbits, but this is incidental to the story in which they also are a flower and gardener, a fish and a fisherman, etc. The story is not about rabbits but is about security and love between a mother and her "child".

- Some topics of interest to three-year-olds are:
  - Those that involve them as naturalists and observers (stories about animals, gardens, plants, flowers, splashing through puddles, collecting stones and shells, caring for living things, etc.).
  - Those that involve them as explorers of their environments (stories about the neighborhood and community helpers; concepts about objects such as fast/slow, hard/soft; transportation vehicles; outings such as going to the library, grocery store, or zoo).
  - Those that involve them as members of their families (stories about mothers and fathers, brothers and sisters, grandparents, babysitters, a new baby, pets, etc.).
  - Those that involve themselves (stories about their senses and their bodies; the clothing they wear and the foods they eat; the emotions they feel such as anger or fears, or how it feels to have a new baby brother or sister; and what they were like when they were a baby).

---

[5]There are several resources that provide names of books, poems, recordings, etc. suitable for storytimes for preschoolers. One excellent source is Margaret Read MacDonald's *Booksharing: 101 Programs to Use with Preschoolers* (Hamden, Conn.: Library Professional Publications, 1988).

During *programs for parents, teachers, and caregivers,* librarians should provide practical literature-centered ideas, such as:

- Presenting and discussing a varied selection of picture books appropriate for three-year-olds.

- Presenting and discussing a selection of resource books featuring poetry, songs, finger plays, nursery rhymes, flannel board stories, and listings of picture books.

- Demonstrating, as often as possible, "how to do" techniques (such as how to do finger plays, or how to read picture books with a group) and "how to make" ideas (such as how to make a flannel board out of heavy cardboard covered with flannel, or how to make figures for the flannel board drawn on and cut out of felt or pictures from magazines with strips of sandpaper glued on the backs, or how to make homemade books and albums).

The following is a list of suggestions and motivating explanations that should be given to parents, teachers, and caregivers:

- Read to the children often, establishing a routine time and place for reading together in addition to impromptu reading times. Let the child sit in the adult's lap during one-to-one storytimes. Remember, however, to keep book activities to the length of the children's interest; do not turn them into long, tiring sessions.

- Understand that children differ greatly, and it is up to the adult to discover which books will be best for the children. Start with a list of recommended titles, but do not force a book if the child seems uninterested.

- Read stories which are being heard for the first time slowly and clearly to allow the children time to assimilate the meaning of the words and to connect the pictures with the text.

- Use voice inflection to enliven the story but not to the extent that it distracts from the story.

- Provide a routine to ensure that even the shy or nonverbal child has an opportunity to talk. Be good listeners by accepting what the children say and in the way they say it, by not making critical remarks that may inhibit the children from speaking, and by issuing well-deserved praise when appropriate. Value the questions asked by the children since they are evidence of the child's mental activity.

- Encourage the children to "read" on their own. Have books accessible to share for casual and frequent use.

- Involve the children with the story activity. Let children select the books they want read. When reading to one child, ask the child to turn the pages as the adult reads. Have children participate in the telling of a story they are familiar with. After the story, ask questions about the pictures, and encourage preschoolers to talk about their own experiences and feelings as they relate to the story.

- Let the children retell a story in their own words and/or actions. When children dramatize stories or poems they have listened to, the vocabulary and the storyline are reinforced. Retelling a familiar story or poem by placing characters and objects on a flannel board is very enjoyable since it shows off the child's increased dexterity and memory.

- Help the children use correct language. You should refrain from repeating or encouraging baby talk; baby talk does not help develop language for the child and is amusing only to the adult.

- Let the children provide the text for wordless picture books. To "read" such a book one may say to the child: "There are no letters and words in this book but there is a story in the pictures." You would then use a finger to direct the child's vision to the left side of the page to start the story, and accept everything the child says about the pictures.

- Introduce books about basic concepts such as color, size and shape, and the alphabet to the child. A preschooler needs early exposure to letters and numbers, which will come to have meaning for him or her with the passage of time.

- Be prepared to reread stories or to repeat activities, such as a finger play or song, that are the children's favorites. Not only does the child have and express preferences, but he or she enjoys repetition. In a world that is changing so quickly for a three-year-old, a favorite, familiar story or poem provides security and comfort because it has no surprises.

- Let the children become aware of the reading process by occasionally following the text with your index finger. This lets children see that letters and words make up written language.

- Help the children understand the mechanics of using books by, for example, showing how to hold and correctly turn the pages of books, how words are ordered from left to right and from the top to the bottom of the page, and how to select a book and return it to the shelf or book box.

- Provide musical and spoken recordings for the children. Favorite songs and stories include those with repeated language phrases, songs with rhyme, those that have silly words, and those that are about babies, the family, machines, pets, etc.

- Provide cassettes and books for children to use on their own. Ideally each child should have a copy of the book since the skill of reading the pictures and turning the pages at the right time develops at different rates among children.

- Share stories that will expose children to a wide variety of topics they can comprehend. They are continually asking "why?" because they are curious about their world. The child can participate in simple experiences that provide a foundation for further knowledge. For example, a rock collection along with a simple book about rocks exposes the child to geology. Adults need to develop an awareness of their children's particular curiosities and then follow-up with experiences that stimulate and reward curiosity.

- Tolerate the errors in children's thinking since errors are often logical extensions of firmly held assumptions.[6]

- Be aware that egoism, the deliberate and fully conscious decision to put one's interests ahead of others, is very different from egocentricism, which is the inability to consider a point of view that is different from one's own point of view. Adults who understand the concept of ego-centricism are more likely to see the child's behavior as a part of a system waiting to be reorganized rather than as a mistake that must be eliminated.

- Engage in matching and naming activities with the children. A game in which the child matches pictures and then says or hears an adult say the name of the picture is a good example. Lotto cards or pictures cut from two copies of the same magazine can be used. This activity will give children a chance to look at pictures carefully and to recognize those that are alike, and to name or hear the names of items in the pictures.

- Transcribe stories which the children dictate. A child who dictates to an adult feels that what he or she has to say is important because an adult is interested enough to write it down. The preschooler's self-confidence expands, and so does his or her interest in words. Reread the story at a later time. Encourage children to see themselves as writers.

- Create books out of inexpensive magnetic photo albums. Favorite pictures from gift catalogs, labels from cans of food the child likes, photographs of special people or places, leaves from a tree in the neighborhood, postcards from friends, and drawings can be placed in an album. These help the child collect things that tell about himself or herself and let the child feel pride. Moreover, these created books are interesting to the child because their contents are known

---

[6]Piaget helped us figure out what some of these assumptions are. For example, for a three-year-old the number "five" is the name of the fifth object and even if it is moved to first place, it still should be called "five."

and prized, and affection for them is transferable to books in general.

- Provide an orderly and well-organized environment which stimulates the children with a variety of books and toys (blocks, puzzles, dolls, etc.), and allow time for their use. Designate a place for books. In a preschool, a cozy book corner where books can be displayed is ideal. Some books should reflect the interests of the children and others should be selected to stimulate them and challenge them to further investigation.

- Use a flannel board to create games that include matching, one-to-one correspondence, and ordering pieces by size, color, or shape. In addition, many stories and related activities lend themselves to the use of a flannel board when the story is reread or retold by an adult or child.

- Recognize that sex roles constitute a classification scheme for the preschooler. It is the first step toward an adult view of what is male and what is female and is heavily influenced by the child's limited classification ability. With time and role models, children are able to see middle ranges of behavior. Stories with characters depicting non-stereotypical sex roles may help the child.

- Realize that children's interest in hearing about babyhood, either in general or about their own, is in part a result of their attempt to establish two separate periods in life. Preschoolers are beginning to deal with the concept of time as something which is abstracted from personal experience. Photograph albums containing baby photos or pictures from magazines are fun to make. Using a flannel board, an adult could show pictures of babies drinking from bottles and eating baby food in contrast to pictures of favorite foods of three-year-olds. This helps the child establish the two times. Picture books that describe what children do as babies and what they do when older are suggested.

- Realize that children need to make discoveries about their world firsthand; it is not enough for them to look at pictures in books. As children handle materials in their play, experiment with equipment, make discoveries and visit places of interest, they reach out with their senses in an attempt to understand their surroundings. Books are ideal tools for supplementing and reinforcing direct experiences, not substitutes for them.

- Let the children see them reading. Adults who look at books, comment about pictures or words in books, and use books as reference sources serve as models for their children. In addition, children will come to see that books are read both for fun and to find out information.

- Visit the public library on a regular basis with the children and check out books and recordings for them. The children will enjoy the outing and the idea of an adventure with an adult. Such visits reinforce the social aspects of books and reading.

- While at the library, allow ample time for the children to select books. It takes time for them to make decisions. If a child is having a difficult time, lay four or five books (which the librarian will be happy to recommend) on a child-sized table and tell the child to select the ones he or she wants to borrow.

- Have a special place at home or at the preschool for library books, and keep them separate from personally owned books. This will help children learn that library books are borrowed, returned to the library, and then replaced by other library books.

Four Years of Age: Developmental Characteristics

Language Development

- By and large, their articulation is no longer infantile. Even though four-year-olds have yet to master many aspects of language, they have little trouble describing situations and their thoughts. The average four-year-old has as many as 1,550 words at her or his command; by four-and-a-half years, this goes up to around 1,900 words.

- Talking may continue to be more important than listening, but to a lesser extent than when they were three.

- Their recitation of the alphabet and numbers continue to be by rote.

- They delight in the sound and patterns of language, such as alliteration and onomatopoeia, in chants, nonsense words, riddles, simple tongue twisters, and cumulative tales.

- They enjoy playing with language, whispering, shouting, and bossing; they make up their own words.

- Children grasp the power of words, and boast, brag, exaggerate, prevaricate, and swear. They may use over and over any word which elicits a strong reaction out of adults.

- They continue to question in earnest, and will ask why, how, what, when.

- They are mastering the use of space words, such as back, front, under, over, in, on, and behind.

- They continue to accompany their every action with running commentary, which is especially noticeable in play and drawing activities.

- They use language to defend their inabilities ("That's too hard.") and to give self-praise ("I did that myself.").

- They learn to sing on pitch, and, with their ability to remember words, enjoy singing alone or in a group.

Intellectual Development

- They remain prelogical or "preoperational" throughout the preschool period. The fact that a four-year-old's language is sophisticated does not mean he or she is very logical. Listening carefully to a child's language or asking questions often reveals gaps between his or her speaking and thinking.

- They are becoming slightly more flexible or "decentered" so that their perceptions are becoming a bit less fixed.

- They are able to understand the difference between what is real and what is imagined when it is carefully explained by an adult. They are also beginning to talk about imaginary conditions ("suppose that...").

- They develop an interest in knowing more about kinds of families and communities other than their own.

- They continue to be extremely curious about people, events, and things around them, and ask many questions. Children are especially curious about their natural and material environment, such as seasonal changes, the sky, tools and machinery, and plants and animals.

- They have more patience when listening to stories in larger groups over longer periods than they did when they were three.

- They enjoy listening to music and making music with their voices, hands, and feet, or by playing percussion instruments or toys.

- They experience growing conceptualization: the four-year-old begins to be able to classify, compare, and order objects according to some property which he or she perceives to be common.

- They are able to replicate the order of a set of objects, such as differently colored or shaped beads, as presented in a model. They can also match simple geometrical shapes.

- They enjoy experimenting with cause-effect and means-end relationships.

- They discover the observable properties of objects and physical phenomena, such as what happens when a marble is released on an incline, by acting on objects and observing the reactions. Four-year-olds drop, squeeze, fold, tap, etc., objects to find out how they respond.

- They see an object as a whole and have difficulty seeing the relationships among the parts.

- They are curious to know more about their own bodies and how they work, such as how the body digests food, eliminates waste, breathes air, circulates blood, and experiences sensations (seeing, hearing, touching, tasting, and smelling). Four-year-olds may also be interested in knowing about reproduction and death.

- They are developing a sense of time and begin to use words and phrases like days, months, minutes, time to go home, correctly.

- They begin to realize that time is a continuum and to understand that people existed and events took place before now and will after now. Children are curious about when a grandparent was a child.

- At age four-and-a-half, they tend to be more self-motivated and are able to stay longer at tasks.

Motor Development

- They appear to have boundless energy and may attempt physical feats that are reckless; they continue to be physically active.

- They easily ascend or descend short steps using alternate feet and are balanced enough to stand on one foot from two to seven seconds.

- They catch a small ball with their elbows in front of their bodies.

- They are able to put on and take off clothes which have zippers or large buttons and are laid out and correctly oriented; four-year-olds may still have trouble telling front from back.

- They wash their hands and face and brush their teeth and hair.

- They may be able to use roller skates and learn to ride a small bicycle with training wheels.

- They enjoy their new abilities and like to try out physical stunts by combining running, climbing, and jumping. Children enjoy gross motor play both outdoors (jungle gym, slides, sand piles) and indoors (big blocks).

- They continue to enjoy moving their bodies to music. This helps them understand the meaning of concept words such as high, low, behind, under, slow, and fast.

- Their coordination has improved so that they delight in building with tinker toys, legos, snap blocks, or bristle blocks.

- At age four, they can draw the picture of a human figure with head, body, arms and legs; at four-and-a-half, they add eyes, hair, ears, hands, and feet to the drawing.

- They enjoy painting, coloring and drawing, and cutting on a line with scissors. Children can make designs and experiment with shape, line, color, and pattern.

- By age four-and-a-half, preschoolers' growing interest in written language and their increased fine motor skills may enable them to print their first names, and some letters and numerals.

Emotional and Personality Development

- Since the sense of initiative continues to dominate, four-year-olds consider it more important to get things started than to finish. Planning and exploring are the essence of the preschool period. They will be much more concerned about finishing jobs and doing them well in the stage which follows (the development of a sense of industry).

- At age four, they seem to be emotionally secure and comfortable, so much so that they boast and brag about how superior they and their family are.

- They have self-confidence and love adventure so that they are willing to try a variety of new tasks. Children take pride in their abilities.

- They experience emotional extremes, laughing and crying loudly even on mild provocation. A child can be charming and beguiling at one moment, obnoxious the next.

- They continue to have fantastic fears and nightmares of monsters, water, large animals, the dark, being sucked down drains in toilets and bathtubs, etc.

- A four-year-old continues to be mostly egocentric but, through encouragement, a child is able to think about people from other households much like his or her own. With time and experience, the preschooler is ready to consider people from households quite different from his or her own.

- They appear to appreciate boundaries set by adults. Children welcome someone who can set limits for their almost boundless energy and daring. They continue to thrive in a structured environment with daily routines.

- At age four-and-a-half, as they become more aware of authority, their awareness of "good" and "bad" increases. Children delight in hearing true stories, either about themselves or their parents, and enjoy stories about how bad or good their parents were when they were little.

Social Development

- They continue to learn many skills from parents, other important adults, siblings, and other children.

- The four-year-old becomes increasingly aware of roles, such as his or her role as an individual, family memberships, or career roles.

- Their increasing motor abilities make home life easier; children can feed themselves, except for cutting, and can talk and eat.

- They experience a widened world if and when they enter a preschool. Whether or not their development is served depends largely on the fit between them and their preschool.

- At preschool, the four-year-old strongly identifies with the group, loves parties and celebrations, and enjoys eating with others.

- They may develop sudden new and intense likes and dislikes for specific people, foods, clothing, toys, etc. for no apparent reason.

- They can play cooperatively with other children.

- They show enthusiasm and willingness to be with play-mates, enjoy the challenge that other children offer, and chatter endlessly when playing together.

- They have limited ability to play games with rules since they have difficulty understanding game rules; egocentricism is still strong. A four-year-old is happiest when he or she is the winner and does not find it illogical for all participants to be winners.

- They continue to delight in play, which takes a variety of forms and can serve many purposes. Initial exploration designed to find out what an unfamiliar object or toy does is called functional play. Constructive play follows when the child actually plays and puts the knowledge gained in exploring to use. Dramatic play, which requires a more complex story line and usually contains elements in the past or future, is less common than other types of play but becomes more frequent among the older four-year-olds.

- They enter into dramatic play and "decenter" or see things from points of view other than their own. For example, a child playing house has to decenter in order to relate to a baby doll from a mother's point of view. The play may be highly elaborate, with members of the group becoming, say, mother, father, storekeeper, astronaut, fire fighter, doctor; and it may be hectic and uncontrolled in its wild shifts of place, pace, and characters.

- They continue to enjoy playing with simple hand puppets alone or within a group.

- They spend a lot of time playing with blocks, sand and water, and dolls and action figures.

- They continue to enjoy circle and simple movement games, especially those that can "trick" them, such as "Simon says" or "telephone" games where a message is whispered from one child to the next.

- The four-year-old plays with a group of three to five other children well. There is less fighting over toys as the child learns to take turns with toys and leadership.

- They may include imaginary playmates in play. Although incomprehensible to adults, they are ideal companions who are always around when wanted, never fight, and agree to every suggestion the child makes.

Four Years of Age: Implications for Library Programs

Library programs for four-year-olds include both storytimes for the children and programs designed for parents and other adults who care for and teach children. As for three-year-olds, serious effort should be made to reach and introduce literature-centered informational programs to those adults who have lengthy contact with children in preschools.

Librarians planning *storytimes* for four-year-olds should find the following list of suggestions helpful:

- The library should be an inviting place for preschoolers to visit. It can be decorated at children's eye level with realistic pictures of people's faces, friendly animals, children playing and cooperating, children and their families, especially those of various cultures, and familiar objects; with child-sized furniture; and with interesting displays.

- Children of this age can sit for longer time periods before becoming fidgety. However, the pace should continue to be quick, and activities that involve the children, such as finger plays, marching to music, creative dramatics, and singing should be included.

- Depending on prior social and storytime experiences, children may be able to sit through and enjoy hearing stories without the use of visuals, such as study prints, book illustrations, or flannel board figures. Tell the stories slowly and clearly, and be certain to give each child eye contact during the story.

- For the child, talking may be more important than listening, so continue to be patient but firm when the preschooler interrupts.

- When several children in a group are eager to talk, help them remember that they must take turns in speaking.

- Encourage children to respect the feelings of other children and to listen to others when they are talking. This helps the children to be aware of different points of view.

- Allow children to engage in word play by repeating refrains in stories and other activities. This practice can build listening skills since children must listen and be ready when it is time to say the refrain.

- In order to encourage language development, speak clearly to children and listen to their responses. During conversations before and after storytimes, face the child and give full attention to the conversation. Squatting or kneeling to the same level as the child helps both the adult and child to communicate.

- Inasmuch as the four-year-old's ability to distinguish the real from the unreal is still developing, imaginative stories should be introduced with careful consideration given to helping the children realize the distinction between what is *real* and what is *pretend*.

- Help children understand how to interpret pictures they are looking at. Ask the children to discuss what is happening in the picture.

- Provide parents, teachers, and caregivers with details about the books and activities by distributing booklists or printed handouts of finger plays, poems, etc. so that they can reread the books and repeat the activities with their children later.

In selecting stories and activities for four-year-olds, the list offered above for three-year-olds should be consulted. Stories and activities listed there will also interest a four-year-old, but for a shorter period of time. Since the child has more breadth of experience and is able to assimilate ideas more rapidly, he or she is ready for somewhat longer, more complicated material:

- Stories and activities that contain more sophisticated language patterns, such as alliteration and onomatopoeia, as displayed in chants, rhyming poetry, nonsense words, riddles, and simple tongue twisters.

- The longer, more complex Mother Goose verses, such as the entire "Old Mother Hubbard," or some of the less well-known verses, such as "If All the Seas Were One Sea."

- Simple, straightforward imaginary stories and activities which do not abruptly jump from one realm to another, but provide a slow transition into fantasy.

- Stories and activities that depict a variety of ages, cultures, and kinds of families in a positive way.

- Stories told without visuals that are short, contain repetition, and have few characters. Stories with short introductions, lots of action, and quick endings are popular.

- Well-known folktales, such as the simple talking animal tales, cumulative tales, and humorous tales. Cumulative ones continue to be favorites. Most of the *pourquoi* tales and fairy tales are better suited for older groups.

- Stories and activities which are well-known to the children and which they can dramatize. For those who are not ready for creative drama, the use of puppets is suggested since the child can take on a number of roles without feeling shy or embarrassed.

- Simple games like "Simon says." They are a good way of practicing motor skills and fitting actions with verbal instructions, and children enjoy them.

- Stories and activities about topics that interest four-year-olds. The cautions about selecting topics for three-year-olds mentioned earlier also apply here. Topics of interest to three-year-olds are also of interest to four-year-olds. Some additional topics are:
  - Those that involve them as more sophisticated naturalists and observers (stories about the sky and its features, physical features of the earth, and seasonal changes).
  - Those that involve them as explorers of concepts (stories about different points in time, which can be recent history found in books by Virginia Lee Burton; letters and numbers; birthdays and other cycle events.)
  - Those that involve them as members of their families and their culture (stories about the role of a child as distinct from that of adults; playing and working cooperatively; the childhood of older adults such as grandparents; and rituals of their culture held on special days).
  - Those that involve other families and other cultures (stories about different kinds of families, homes, customs, and rituals of various cultures).

During *programs for parents, teachers, and caregivers,* librarians should provide practical literature-centered ideas, such as:

- Presenting and discussing a varied selection of picture books appropriate for four-year-olds.

- Presenting and discussing a selection of resource books featuring poetry, songs, finger plays, nursery rhyme books, and listings of picture books.

- Demonstrating, as often as possible, "how to do" techniques (such as how to do finger plays or read picture books to a group) and "how to make" ideas (such as how to make a flannel board and figures for flannel board use or how to make homemade books and albums).

When providing suggestions and explanations to parents, teachers, and caregivers during *informational programs*, the list offered above for three-year-olds should be consulted. These will also be appropriate for four-year-olds. In addition, that list should be augmented with the following list of suggestions just for four-year-olds:

- Let the children listen to and "write" tongue twisters, simple riddles, and chants. The writing can be done by the listening adult.

- Recognize that activities designed solely to teach the alphabet or numbers are much less appropriate than providing a print-rich environment that stimulates language.

- Continue to recite nursery rhymes with the children. Even though the rhymes seem illogical to adults, remember that logic is not the preschooler's strong suit. Nursery rhymes let them play with funny, nonsensical language.

- Help children become better observers of nature by showing them the importance of observing before acting. Books such as Marie Hall Ets's *Play with Me* help children learn the important concept of being a quiet observer, not a possessor or a destroyer.

- Encourage children to see relationships among the many observations they make in nature and in picture books. For example, when a child observes in a picture that it is raining, the adult can comment that the rain will help the flower seeds grow into plants. However, it is important to point out the gross relationships rather than the subtle ones which are appropriate for older children.

- Read informational books, avoiding ones that obscure the basic facts by use of anthropomorphism or excessive embellishment. Children are fascinated with their physical world and themselves; they need only the facts.

- Expose the children to different illustrative interpretations of familiar folk tales, such as Paul Galdone and William Stobbs's versions of *Three Billy Goats Gruff.* This will help children see that there is not just one way to draw pictures for a story.

- Use flannel boards to create a story situation in which two groups of objects, such as various farm animals and various transportation vehicles, can be first mixed-up then sorted according to their similarities. This helps develop the children's ability to find similarities and differences among objects.

- Capitalize on the growing interest the children have in their bodies by reading informational books that introduce simple concepts needed to understand biological processes such as digestion, excretion, respiration, circulation, reproduction, and death. Helping children form correct concepts early can forestall anxieties and fears that may arise when they pick up misconceptions from friends or from half-heard conversations.

- Provide ample opportunities for the children to color, draw, "write", and cut. Cutting a picture into parts and then putting it together again, puzzle fashion, is suggested. Respect children's "writing" and scribbling since those marks may be much more than random squiggles for the child.

- Recognize the great importance of play. Imaginative play can transform the world the preschooler sees and recreate it in miniature. It is one way the child comprehends the world.

- Provide the children with simple hand puppets and time for their use since they encourage creative play. A simple puppet stage made from a large appliance carton with a rectangular opening cut out of it encourages puppet play.

- Provide musical activities. Children enjoy responding rhythmically to live and recorded music. As children acquire increasing control over their bodies, musical experiences can be expressive and interpretive rather than imitative of someone else's motions.

- Visit the public library on a regular basis with the children and check out books and recordings, paying attention to the many excellent informational books and simple folktales and imaginary stories that are of interest to four-year-olds.

These library activities which correspond to the developmental characteristics of three- and four-year-olds should be taken as just a starting point by children's librarians. It is the author's hope that this information will help librarians find materials which are tailored to the needs and interests of the preschoolers with whom they are working, either directly through storytimes or indirectly through programs for adults.

Program Considerations: Multicultural Education and Preschoolers with Special Needs

Multicultural Education

AS PRESCHOOLERS develop social skills, they are learning more about relationships between themselves and their environment —as members of family groups and of a wider community. Books and media can play an important role in bringing an understanding of the wider community to children, which is vital in this country with its broad range of ethnic and cultural groups and the constant stream of new immigrants.

Multicultural education allows children to develop an awareness of different cultures and ethnic groups in the hope that they will gain an understanding and acceptance of their own culture and the culture of others. Learning to be a member of a multicultural society involves being able to recognize that there are both similarities and differences among all groups of people, including one's own family and friends. That one is able to demonstrate an acceptance of and a respect for various ethnic groups and cultures is an important objective of an educational program.

One early childhood education source states that in order to implement an effective multicultural program, the planners should include the following overall goals:

117

1. To recognize that children from all cultures have similar needs and that every person is unique.

2. To help develop a positive self-concept in the child by exploring the cultural backgrounds of the children.

3. To provide a foundation that instills in the child a sense of dignity and tolerance.

4. To increase the knowledge and understanding the child has about his or her own cultural and ethnic heritage and that of other children.

5. To explore the family composition, customs, living conditions, and lifestyles of children and families in cultures.

6. To provide the support for adopted or foster children to develop a sense of heritage.

7. To recognize individual differences within a cultural or ethnic group.

8. To assist children and families who are new to the United States with transitions to a new and different culture.[1]

Multicultural education in general should not be viewed as a separate program or set of activities that is added on to an existing program. Nor should it be viewed as the study of isolated cultures. Instead, it should be seen as a perspective that becomes a part of a curriculum or program.

This is especially true for library programs. Books and media that help preschoolers develop an awareness and acceptance of their own families and cultures along with the cultures of others need to be integrated throughout library programs. This is just as important in monocultural communities as it is in communities with diverse ethnic and cultural groups.

Books and media can never substitute for first-hand contact preschoolers need to have with other people, but they can serve as vehicles that introduce and reinforce multicultural awareness.

---

[1]Claudia F. Eliason and Loa T. Jenkins, *A Practical Guide to Early Childhood Curriculum*, 3rd. ed. (Columbus, Ohio: Merrill, 1986), 36–7.

Librarians interested in encouraging preschoolers to become more culturally aware should find the following lists of suggestions helpful:

When selecting materials for preschoolers, look for those that

• recognize both similarities and differences of ethnic groups and cultures;

• reflect the pluralistic nature of our society, both past and present;

• portray children and adults, whatever their cultures, displaying various human emotions, both negative and positive;

• avoid stereotypes in illustration and text (especially dialect);

• are considered authentic by members of the cultural or ethnic group that is depicted.

When planning programs for preschoolers and adults, learn as much as possible about the cultural and ethnic backgrounds of the audience. Then,

• in addition to obvious characteristics such as language, folklore, foods, games, clothing, and music, learn about other characteristics of the groups, such as the emphasis placed on family-ties, traditions, education, or leisure activities;

• include books and media which present similarities and differences among families and people in a positive fashion that may help preschoolers learn to respect and accept their *own* culture;

• include books and media which present similarities and differences among families and people in a positive fashion that may help preschoolers learn to respect and accept others *outside* their culture.

- broaden the cultural basis to include books and media depicting different types of clothing, languages, music, housing, and foods;
- include books and media about less well-known holidays from other cultures in addition to the traditional, better-known ones.

During storytimes, librarians, teachers and caregivers should encourage children to discuss their backgrounds. In this way children may become aware that other children in their own community are from families who have come here from various countries.

Preschoolers with Special Needs

Most children will have special needs from time to time, but some require specialized attention more consistently. Children who have speech, language, mental, or emotional delays, and those who are visually, hearing, or physically impaired make up the latter group.

In the early part of this century Maria Montessori devised educational methods and materials for the young slum children in Rome because she observed that children from poor homes did not develop normally.[2] In the early 1930s the landmark work of Harold Skeels and Howard Dye demonstrated the effects of early stimulation on the development of thirteen children under the age of three who had been diagnosed as mentally retarded and moved from an orphanage to an institution for the mentally retarded. The children received a great amount of attention from older mentally retarded patients and ward attendants. One-and-a-half years later, the thirteen children gained an average of 27.5 IQ points in contrast to an average loss of 26 points for the comparison group of children who remained in the orphanage with limited stimulation. A follow-up study years later revealed that all of the children who were in the experimental group

---

[2]Maria Montessori, *The Montessori Method* (New York: Stokes, 1912).

became self-supporting while those in the comparison group remained either institutionalized or worked at low-level jobs.[3]

Later, in 1948 Samuel Kirk began his landmark five-year study with mentally retarded three- to six-year-olds. There were two groups: one lived in a community and the other in an institution for mentally retarded. Contrast groups were identified from each setting. The experimental groups from both settings were given individualized and small group instruction along with blocks of time for play. Kirk's findings were comparable to those of Skeels and Dye. Seventy percent of the experimental children demonstrated an accelerated rate of development, and a follow-up study showed that they retained the gains over time. The contrast children either maintained or showed a decrease in their rate of development. Moreover, Kirk's study showed that the greater the change in the child's environment, the greater the speed in development. Those who were placed in foster homes and attended preschools, compared to those who stayed in institutions and attended preschools, made greater gains.[4] Kirk's study was one of the first that pointed to the need for intervention in both the home and school settings for optimal development of mentally retarded preschool children.

In the mid-1960s federal funds for disadvantaged children triggered a number of researchers to design center-based programs for young disadvantaged children and their families.[5]

---

[3]Harold M. Skeels and Howard B. Dye, "A Study of the Effects of Differential Stimulation on Mentally Retarded Children," *Proceedings of the Annual Convention of the American Association of Mental Deficiency* 22 (1939): 114–136; and Harold M. Skeels, *Adult Status of Children with Contrasting Early Life Experiences: A Follow-up Study*, Monograph 105, *Monographs of the Society for Research in Child Development* 31, no. 3 (1966).

[4]Samuel A. Kirk, *Early Education of the Mentally Retarded* (Urbana, Ill.: University of Illinois Press, 1958).

[5]Examples include: Bettye M. Caldwell and Julius Richmond, "The Children's Center in Syracuse, New York," in *Early Child Care: The New Perspectives*, edited by Laura Dittmann (New York: Atherton, 1968), 326–358; David Weikart, "Preschool Programs: Preliminary Findings,"

However, it was not until the 1970s that the field of early childhood special education emerged to meet the specific challenge of identifying and helping young children with special needs. Before then special education typically focused on older disabled children and early childhood education typically served normal young children. Federal legislation, research that showed that intervention programs for young children are effective, the belief in the importance of the early childhood years for both normal and disabled children, and effective model early childhood special education programs all aided in the development of this new field.

The Education for All Handicapped Children Act (Public Law 94-142) passed by Congress in 1975 has had a remarkable impact on education for these children. The law required that by September 1980, a free education in the least restrictive environment appropriate to the child's ability should be provided for all disabled children from three to twenty-one years of age. However, if normal children between the ages of three and five are not educated by the state, then the state has no responsibility to educated the disabled children of those ages. This has meant that preschoolers with disabilities are denied public educational services altogether in some states and are provided with services in segregated settings in others since there are no normal children of the same age in the public schools.

The notable place where disabled preschoolers have been and continue to be educated is Head Start programs. After 1970, Head Start centers were required to enroll disabled children as 10 percent of the total enrollment and to offer appropriate educational and medical services for these children. Today, Head Start has become the largest provider of preschool education to children with special needs.[6]

Journal of Special Education 1 (Winter 1967): 163–181; Merle B. Karnes et al., "An Approach for Working Mothers of Disadvantaged Children in the Preschool," _Merrill-Palmer Quarterly_ 14 (April 1968): 174–184.

[6]A. Frederick North, "The Developmentally Disabled Child: Preventive Efforts and Governmental Programs," in _Child Development and Developmental Disabilities_, ed. Stewart Gabel and Marilyn T. Erickson

Mainstreaming

Mainstreaming is the integration of disabled children into educational settings containing mainly normal children. The courts have supported the move to mainstream disabled children, identifying their right to a free public education in the least restricted educational setting and the right of their parents to review educational decisions about them.[7]

It should be noted, however, that Public Law 94-142, which caused mainstreaming to come about on a national level, did not mean that special education programs should be abandoned and that the disabled would be integrated randomly into regular classrooms. It meant that disabled children would be entitled to receive an education in the least restrictive environment where they were able to learn.

According to research by Spodek, Saracho, and Lee there is often no academic advantage to placing mildly to moderately disabled preschoolers in segregated settings. Furthermore, the social behavior of most disabled children more closely approximates those of normal peers when they are together. Finally, mainstreaming may benefit all children by developing an awareness of and respect for individual differences without any loss in academic achievement.[8]

Characteristics of Disabled Children

Librarians who work with disabled preschoolers must seek out information about the child's particular condition if they want

---

(Boston: Little, Brown, 1980), 482–83. In his discussion North points out that the severity of the disabilities of the children enrolled (most have speech problems) and the degree to which the services were additional to what was already available in the community served by Head Start are not made clear by the government in its statistics.

[7]Bernard Spodek, *Teaching in the Early Years*, 3rd ed. (Englewood Cliffs, N.J.: Prentice-Hall, 1985), 198–199.

[8]Bernard Spodek, Olivia N. Saracho, and Richard C. Lee, "Mainstreaming Handicapped Children in the Preschool," in *Advances in Early Education and Day Care* (Vol. 3), ed. S. Kilmer, (Greenwich, Conn.: JAI Press, 1983).

to be effective. Information from books, such as Lucas and Karrenbrock's *The Disabled Child in the Library*,[9] or from associations and agencies, such as the Easter Seal Society (70 East Lake Street, Chicago, IL 60601; phone: 312-726-6200), the Epilepsy Foundation of America (4351 Garden City Drive, Landover, MD 20785; phone: 301-459-3700), the American Council for the Blind (1010 Vermont Avenue N.W., Suite 1100, Washington, D.C. 20005; phone: 202-393-3666), the American Foundation for the Blind (15 West 16th Street, New York, NY 10011; phone: 212-620-2000 and toll-free hot line: 800 AFB-LIND), the Association for Children and Adults with Learning Disabilities (4156 Library Road, Pittsburgh, PA 15234; phone: 412-341-1515), or the United Cerebral Palsy Association (7 Penn Plaza, Suite 804, New York, NY 10001; phone: 212-268-6655), are useful, if not vital, in understanding the nature of specific disabilities.

The majority of disabilities can be categorized as physical or motor problems, mental retardation, learning disabilities, behavior disabilities, visual and hearing impairments, and communication disorders. Readers should realize that this section which briefly describes the general characteristics of these disabilities does nothing more than scratch the surface.

CHILDREN WITH PHYSICAL OR MOTOR PROBLEMS

These children have functional restrictions on their physical abilities, such as mobility, hand use, body control, or strength and stamina. The restriction interferes to the point that services such as training, equipment, materials, or facilities are required. Among the most common conditions that librarians will see are spina bifida, cerebral palsy, sickle cell anemia, muscular dystrophy, and epilepsy.

Spina bifida occurs when the spinal column is not fully developed and does not completely enclose the spinal cord. The

---

[9]Linda Lucas and Marilyn H. Karrenbrock, *The Disabled Child in the Library: Moving into the Mainstream* (Littleton, Col.: Libraries Unlimited, 1983).

young child has fewer problems when there is no deformity of the spinal cord. However, if part of the spinal cord protrudes through an opening, there are more problems. Children with spina bifida may have motor impairment in addition to a lack of bowel and bladder control.

Cerebral palsy occurs as a result of injury to the brain before, during or after birth. It is a neuromuscular disability which in most cases has no direct effect on the learning capability of the child. In mild cases, the young child may appear awkward or clumsy, or may talk more slowly than others. In moderate to severe cases, the young child may have spasticity (muscular tightness and difficulty in moving), athetosis (uncontrollable rhythmic movement in the muscles), and ataxia (lack of muscle coordination and balance).

Sickle-cell anemia is a genetic disorder that is commonly found in African-Americans. It results in a distortion and malfunction of red blood cells which reduce a child's supply of oxygen. During a crisis period, the child experiences severe pain which is very difficult to relieve even when the child is hospitalized and given drugs.

Muscular dystrophy is a muscular disease which is progressive. It results in increasing muscular weakness and uncoordination. Preschoolers with muscular dystrophy will probably have a limited life span, usually dying before their twentieth birthday.

Epilepsy is a brain disorder which produces periods of abnormal changes in electrical brain patterns that trigger seizures. Young children with epilepsy may experience so-called *petit mal* seizures which result in loss of consciousness for a brief time and are not always noticed or mistaken for inattentiveness. *Grand mal* seizures result in loss of consciousness for more extended periods of time. Seizure patterns vary greatly among children. Medication is nearly always helpful in controlling seizures.

Children with physical problems usually have difficulty with social interactions, mobility, self-help skills, and, frequently, proper speech. For many of these children their receptive language is much better than their expressive language, and librarians may often wrongly assume that these children know less than they actually do.

CHILDREN WITH MENTAL RETARDATION

The problem of defining and describing mental retardation has plagued special educators for many years. Traditionally and in many current classifications, retardation and the levels of retardation are measured only by intelligence testing. Today, some organizations define it in terms of deficiencies in adaptive behavior measures as well as intelligence. Adaptive behavior means the degree to which the child can meet age level standards of self-sufficiency. One classification is as follows:

- *Educable mentally retarded* (EMR), defined as those with an IQ of 50 to 75/80, who are often candidates for mainstreaming, and have potentialities in academic subjects, social adjustment, and minimal occupational adequacies.

- *Trainable mentally retarded* (TMR), defined as those with an IQ of 25/30 to 49, who are not educable in the traditional sense but have potentialities for training in self-help skills, social adjustment in the family life, and economic usefulness.

- *Severely mentally retarded* (SMR), defined as those with an IQ of 25/30 and lower, who are unable to be trained in total self-care, socialization, or economic usefulness, and require almost complete care and supervision throughout life.[10]

LEARNING DISABLED CHILDREN

The premise of mental retardation is that the child lacks the capacity to learn what a normal child can learn. On the other hand, the notion of learning disabilities is based on the premise that there is a discrepancy between the child's capacity and his

---

[10]G. Maxim, *The Very Young: Guiding Children from Infancy through the Early Years*, 2nd ed. (Belmont, Cal.: Wadsworth, 1985), 450.

actual academic achievement. At times there is a fine line between labeling a child mildly retarded or learning disabled.

Definitions for learning disabled are both complicated and inadequate. Generally, this group includes children with both neurological and functional impairments. Specific disorders are hyperactivity; perceptual-motor impairment; impulsivity; disabilities in memory and conceptual thinking; speech and hearing disorders; and neurological problems such as cerebral palsy or epilepsy.

BEHAVIORALLY DISABLED CHILDREN

Behavioral disorders, also called emotional disturbances, may be defined as deviations from typical age-appropriate behavior that significantly interfere with the child's own development or with the lives of others.[11] Behaviorally disabled children may seem strange: they may be very aggressive or very shy, very loud or very quiet, very euphoric or very depressed.

Once again, there is no agreement among educators about what constitutes this disability, but behaviorally disabled children often have a number of behaviors that occur at a much greater frequency than with normal children. Behaviors include such things as temper tantrums, head banging, inability to deal with frustration, moodiness, aggressiveness, fearfulness, and withdrawal.

All preschoolers exhibit some inappropriate behaviors at some time or another. In small amounts or for short periods of time, these behaviors are typical. However, the behaviorally disabled child differs from the normal child in the severity of the behavior, the length of time over which the behavior occurs, and where and when the behavior occurs. Behaviorally disabled children exhibit maladaptive behaviors that occur throughout the day and continue for extended periods of time with no sign of lessening without proper help.

---

[11]Bernard Spodek, Olivia N. Saracho, and Richard C. Lee, *Mainstreaming Young Children* (Belmont, Cal.: Wadsworth, 1984), 12.

CHILDREN WITH VISUAL IMPAIRMENTS

A child is considered visually impaired when his or her eyes do not function to allow normal sight in at least one eye. Visual impairment is usually caused by a malfunction of the eye or optic nerve.

Blindness is commonly thought of as a total lack of sight. However, the term includes varying degrees of vision including being able to see objects out of focus or blurred, or being able to see objects only directly ahead as if looking through a hole. Very few children, even those who are considered legally blind, are unable to see at all.

In the legal definition, a person is considered blind if vision in the better eye after correction is 20/200 or worse. A person is considered partially seeing if vision in the better eye after correction is between 20/70 and 20/200. For educational purposes, blindness is not measured by visual acuity but rather by the child's ability to read print. Blind children are those who must be taught to read braille or use devices that do not require sight. Partially sighted children are those who can be taught to read regular or large print materials. They usually need to hold the material very close or to magnify it.

For the visually impaired preschooler with no useful vision, the two options for reading are braille and the optacon. Braille is a touch print medium that uses embossed dots to represent print symbols. Books in braille tend to be large due to the space required to print braille characters and the thickness of paper. The optacon (optical to tactile converter) is an electronic device that translates print into a tactile form which can be felt by the reader's finger. The reader can feel the print as it appears on the page.

The American Brotherhood for the Blind (18440 Oxnard Street, Tarzana, California 91356; phone: 818-343-2022) offers a service called Twin Vision. Twin Vision children's books combine adjacent pages of print and braille so that blind and sighted readers can share books together. Schools and libraries serving the blind usually have copies of Twin Vision books since ABB distributes the books to them. Individual blind children and blind parents of sighted children can receive books from ABB for 90 day loan periods free of charge.

A recent government publication, *R Is for Reading*, is a collection of first-hand accounts from visually impaired children, parents, teachers, reading specialists, child development counselors, and librarians which attempts "to characterize the handicapped juvenile library user and nonuser and to promote some new ideas for serving them among librarians in the NLS (National Library Service for the Blind and Physically Handicapped) network."[12] The interviews offer the librarian suggestions about how to work with parents and children when using braille and cassettes. They also offer insights into the world of the visually impaired child. For example, David Anderson, in "How Blind Children Understand Language," recounts an experience he had to illustrate how a common phrase may mean something quite different to a blind child:

> One day, one of the children I worked with, who was about five years old, was playing and rolling Play-Doh in his hands as we talked about other things. At one point he stopped in the middle of what we were talking about, put the ball of Play-Doh down, and said, "I'll be right back." I said, "Where are you going?" He just repeated, "I'll be right back." But he did not move. He sat there on the floor, picking the Play-Doh from under his fingernails. After a minute or two he said, "I'm back," and picked up the ball of Play-Doh. It occurred to me that he had heard his mom, dad, or others say, "I'll be right back," but never actually experienced their leaving the room.[13]

---

[12]Leslie Eldridge, ed. *R Is for Reading: Library Service to Blind and Physically Handicapped Children* (Washington, D.C.: Library of Congress, National Library Service for the Blind and Physically Handicapped, 1985), 4.

[13]Ibid, 82.

CHILDREN WITH HEARING IMPAIRMENTS

A child is considered hearing impaired when he or she is unable to hear sounds due to a malfunction of the ear or of the associated nerves. The impairment can be temporary or permanent and severe or mild. As in the case of visual impairments, defining hearing impairments is complicated.

Hearing loss is typically measured in intensity and in frequency or pitch of sound that can be heard. The intensity of sounds is measured in decibels, usually in the 0 to 120 decibel range. A child whose hearing test results indicate a loss of 20 to 60 decibels is considered hard of hearing; one with a loss of 60 decibels or more is considered deaf.

If hearing aids are not effective, there are two alternatives to hearing speech which can be used with or without the use of hearing aids, speech reading and manual communication. In speech reading, a person understands by the movement of the speaker's lips, tongue, and face. Speech reading is not, however, an exact process since many sounds (such as bat and pat) look the same to a hearing impaired person. A speech reader must fill in many sounds and words through context cues.

The second major alternative is manual communication which includes sign language and finger spelling. It allows hearing impaired children to both receive and send messages through a system that uses gestures along with hand and finger movements. In the United States today, there are three major sign language systems used, and not all hearing impaired people use the same system. Some use Signing Exact English (SEE), some use American Sign Language (Amsilang), and others use Manual English. The three systems have pronounced differences. Finger spelling, however, with its finger positions representing each letter of the alphabet and number, is standardized. It should be noted that all three signing systems use finger spelling for unfamiliar words, proper names, and for words not available in sign.

CHILDREN WITH COMMUNICATION DISORDERS

Language, according to Hallahan and Kauffman,

> is the communication of ideas through symbols that are used according to semantic and grammatical rules. Thus defined, language includes the sign language of the deaf ... tactile symbols systems (e.g., braille), and conventional written language.... Speech is the behavior of forming and sequencing the sounds of oral language.[14]

Problems with language in this wide sense can occur in those who communicate by gestures, tactile, written, or oral means. We usually think of communication disorders as oral language disabilities, but they do not necessarily have to be so narrowly defined.

Oral language disabilities appear when children do not understand what is spoken to them or when they do not express themselves meaningfully. Therefore, oral language can be divided into receptive factors, or those that involve the ability to understand what is being said and to understand the message, and expressive factors, or those that involve the ability to send an oral message.

Communication disorders in oral language are among the most prevalent problems found in young children. They include the following:

- Articulation disorders (sound substitution, omission, addition, and distortion such as lisping and baby talk).

- Voice problems (excessive nasality or poor nasal emission when speaking, as well as problems of pitch and intensity).

- Stuttering (oscillations, fixations, repetitions, and prolongations of sounds, syllables, words, or phrases).

---

[14]D.P. Hallahan and J.M. Kauffman, *Exceptional Children: Introduction to Special Education* (Englewood Cliffs, N.J.: Prentice-Hall, 1978), 224.

- Cluttering (excessively fast speech, garbled syllables and sounds, disorganized sentence structure, and excessive repetitions).

The severity of the above mentioned communication disorders is questionable in many cases, since many are problems of delayed development that disappear in time. Other problems are not questionable, such as aphasia, which is the partial or total failure of speech to develop. In addition, there are other serious speech problems which are the result of other disorders such as cerebral palsy or cleft palate. Although the common disabilities were described separately above, librarians need to be aware that they do not always occur separately. Some children have multiple disabilities, which tends to complicate diagnosis and remediation. Librarians are urged to read further information about the characteristics of multiple disabled children.

Library Programs for Preschoolers with Special Needs

Library programs for preschoolers with special needs can be designed for the children alone, for the children along with the adults who care for and teach them, or for the adults alone. Programs for preschoolers who come to the library with their parents/caregivers or who are in Head Start and other mainstreamed preschool groups must be adapted to accommodate the extended range of individual differences.

An understanding of typical development, which is offered in the Schema in Chapter 5, is necessary if a librarian is to work effectively among children with special needs and their parents, teachers, and caregivers. This understanding provides a basis upon which to modify library program contents to meet the needs of the preschoolers and guidelines of realistic expectations for all children.

The interests of disabled preschoolers are likely to be the same as those of other preschoolers. Therefore librarians should proceed on the premise that disabled children and normal children gain similar pleasure from similar activities. However, librarians should consider the special needs of children when planning and presenting programs because adaptations to special needs may be required. This may take considerable effort in a group which has children with various disabilities.

Librarians planning programs for preschoolers with special needs should:

- Select physical facilities to accommodate the disability. For orthopedically disabled children, there should be no stairs to impede access. Aisles, including those between book stacks, and door openings need be wide enough for wheelchairs. Spaces for programs should have short napped carpeting, acoustical ceilings and baffles to help reduce distracting noises for hearing impaired and mentally retarded preschoolers.

- Learn about the special needs of the children. For example, Bleck and Nagel's *Physically Handicapped Children: A Medical Atlas for Teachers*[15] is one reference book that contains simple, clear descriptions and diagrams of physical disabilities ranging from heart defects to muscular dystrophy. Most chapters include suggestions on what the teacher should do in the classroom to create the setting most conducive to learning.

- Provide in-service training to library staff involved with the programs so they can understand preschoolers with special needs and their families better.

- Talk with the teachers and parents about the disabled child (but not in front of the child) to be able to assess better any limitations of the child which may influence the library program. Teachers and parents are also excellent sources of practical advice about how to help the child effectively.

- Keep the size of the group small.

---

[15]Eugene E. Bleck and Donald A. Nagel, eds. *Physically Handicapped Children: A Medical Atlas for Teachers*, 2nd ed. (New York: Grune and Stratton, 1982).

- Invite disabled adults to be a part of your program. Perhaps a blind adult could read a Twin Vision book or a deaf adult could sign a well-known nursery rhyme to the group. They serve as high-functioning role models for normal and disabled preschoolers alike.

- Select materials with simple story lines, lots of action and dialog, and little description.

- Include a variety of materials and methods of presentation. Take special needs into account when selecting materials. For example, for hearing impaired preschoolers, select materials which place emphasis on the visual component, such as flannel board stories, pictures, or tell-and-draw stories. Materials that rely heavily on the sound of language should not be used. For blind preschoolers, select materials where the visual component is not indispensable.

- Include real objects and puppets that require the preschoolers to use their senses. For example, if a story or film is about a duck, have the children touch a puppet or stuffed toy duck or a feather after the story. If a poem is about a flower, have a bouquet of flowers that the children can smell after the poem is read.

- Repeat stories and activities as needed. All preschoolers enjoy repetition and mentally retarded preschoolers enjoy and benefit from it even more.

- Include books, songs, poems, and finger plays that expose children to sign language, the fourth most frequently used language in the United States. Perhaps an adult or an older children who knows sign language can sign during the program. Once again, they serve as models for both disabled and normal children.

When presenting programs, librarians should:

- Attempt to see through the disability to the typical in every preschooler. It is easy to get caught up in the differences so that the librarian loses sight that the child is largely like other children in the group and should be treated as much like them as possible. Consistency and reasonable expectations of behavior are, if anything, more important to use when dealing with disabled children than when dealing with normal children.

- Provide short, clear introductions before stories and activities. This is especially helpful to the hearing impaired who lip read since it allows the child a chance to adjust to the librarian's facial and lip patterns.

- Speak clearly with expression and mild gestures but not with over-exaggerated facial or body movements. Librarians may want to speak at a very slightly slower pace, while taking care to retain the rhythm of speech.

- Have children, especially those who are lip reading, at the same eye-level as the speaker. Librarians should speak in a strong, clear light without glare while sitting in low chairs or stools. They should avoid standing or sitting on high stools.

- Provide time for children to look at pictures, either in a book or in flannel board story. This is especially important with children who are lip reading since they need to look away from the speaker's lips in order to look at the visual. It may be difficult for the librarian *not* to speak when he or she wants the preschoolers' attention on the visual.

7

Literature Programs for Preschoolers

Programs for Parents, Teachers, and Caregivers

IF LIBRARIANS are to reach the goal of instilling a love for books and reading in children, we must emphasize programs for parents, teachers, and caregivers of preschoolers. The need for this emphasis stems from the following two premises:

1. As pointed out in the Schema, one of the most important developmental characteristics of preschoolers is their desire for repetition. Preschoolers need to have many books and literature-centered activities shared with them daily. Only parents and others who interact with the children on a frequent, if not daily, basis, such as teachers and caregivers, can provide them with the needed repetition of stories and storytimes.

2. Since librarians cannot reach many, possibly most, of the children in communities at all, librarians should concentrate on reaching and teaching adults the importance of books and reading. The adults, in turn, will read to children in their care and expose them to books, thereby helping to reach the goal.

Many libraries currently offer programs for adults who care for preschoolers. Most programs have four basic objectives:

1. to introduce adults to quality books;

2. to provide criteria for selecting books and literature;

3. to give adults hands-on experience with materials; and

4. to offer suggestions on how to use books and literature with children.

One common format is a workshop where librarians demonstrate storytime techniques, such as how to do finger plays, use a flannel board, and make simple puppets in addition to discussing books which can be found at the library. Other media, such as filmstrips, records, tapes, compact discs, study prints, videos, and films, are also featured if the library loans them. Workshops often focus on discussions of *what* materials are appropriate for young children and *why*.

To provide reinforcement for workshop participants, bibliographies and other handouts are given to the adults. The bibliographies list titles of books and media featured in the workshop along with additional appropriate titles found in the library. Handouts include details of instructions given during the workshop, such as directions for making a simple sock puppet or the words and actions to a finger play. The Schema in Chapter 5 provides practical literature-centered ideas which librarians may want to suggest to parents, teachers, and caregivers during workshops.

Another common format is a demonstration storytime where librarians conduct storytimes for preschoolers with adults in attendance. The rationale for this program is that adults will see how the librarian does a storytime: the librarian reads and shows appropriate books and other materials and models techniques in a realistic setting for adults to observe. During such programs it is vital for adults to pay attention to what and how materials are used instead of paying attention to the children who are participating in the storytime. As in the case of workshops, bibliographies and other handouts should be prepared in advance for adults. The Schema in Chapter 5 provides ideas for materials and techniques that can be used during storytime programs.

Workshops and demonstration storytimes can be conducted inside or outside of the library. To reach the largest number and most diverse range of adults, many librarians take programs out of the library to adult groups. Since many of the participants of the programs conducted outside of the library are not regular library users, librarians must concentrate on the initial contact and the need for establishing a comfortable rapport with the participants. Because the adults range from semi-literate parents and child care personnel to professional educators, the manner of presentation, especially of workshops, needs to be considered and tailored for each group. Any available information about the attendees helps determine the depth and content of the workshop or demonstration storytime.

Reaching Teachers and Caregivers

Librarians must give serious consideration to reaching and teaching adults who provide care for preschoolers outside of the home. The proportion of children under six years of age with mothers who worked outside of the home has increased from 29% in 1970 to 51% in 1988.[1] According to one authority, if the trend continues, just under 15 million children under the age of six will have mothers working outside of the home by 1995. This figure represents two-thirds of the projected preschool population.[2]

One of the most efficient ways of reaching adults who have contact with children is to work with agencies and institutions within the community. Private, employer-supported and religious affiliated child care centers, Head Start programs, parent groups, public and private schools with preschools, agencies that work with disabled preschoolers, and volunteer groups who work in hospitals with children are worth considering. If there are training classes for early childhood care providers at local community colleges, colleges of education, or other formal

---

[1]Sandra Hofferth, "What Is the Demand for and Supply of Child Care in the United States?" *Young Children* 44 (July 1989): 29.
   [2]Ibid.

programs, librarians should contact these groups. Any organization or group that has some type of long-term interaction with preschool children should be considered for cooperation.

If there is a 4C (Community Coordinated Child Development Council) or a chapter of the Association for the Education of Young Children (AEYC) in the area, the library should contact it. Staff from organizations that work with preschools, child care centers, and home day care providers can be emissaries for libraries by including flyers about library service and programs in packets they provide to their clientele.

It is a challenge to many librarians to reach the family day care providers who are often isolated from any type of agency or institution and who seldom, if ever, bring children to the library because of car safety regulations or the spread of drop-off or pick-up times by parents. Local governments of larger communities usually have some type of family day care licensing body under the control of a health or social services licensing department which will mail a listing of licensed family day care homes to the library. It should be realized, however, that in many cases these lists are not up to date.

Brochures advertising the library's programs for teachers and caregivers can be mailed to the preschools, child care centers, and other agencies and institutions. If response is low, a call from librarians to explain the purpose and the contents of the workshop may be in order.

Some libraries have established a line of communication between the library and schools and agencies through regularly issued newsletters. The contents of the newsletters include announcements of special events and workshops that will take place at the library, seasonal and specialized lists of available materials suited for preschoolers, and storytime ideas such as topics and sample finger plays that adults can use with their preschoolers.

Programs for teachers and caregivers in child care centers and preschools publicized in newsletters alerting them to library service and materials foster a solid connection between the centers or preschools and the libraries. In communities where many preschoolers are cared for outside the home, teaching literature-centered techniques and the value of reading to the adults who care for children is the most cost effective way to reach the goal of instilling a love for books and learning in children.

Reaching Parents

Libraries conduct parent programs either for the parents alone or for them with their preschoolers. Some have concurrent programs: storytimes for the preschoolers during which parents are presented with a literature-centered workshop. Others offer workshops for parents where their children sit with them. These programs are not the same as storytimes that include adults. During parent workshops the focus is on introducing a large number books and media to adults, not just the few that are read from cover to cover during preschool storytimes.

In the past, announcements of literature-centered workshops for parents of preschoolers were mailed to parents using mailing lists from area preschools and child care centers. Today, mailing lists are rarely available, and announcements are mailed to preschools and child care centers where they are passed on to the parents. Other sources for disseminating information are the agencies which work with disabled preschoolers and their parents. Some libraries have been successful in reaching parents who are not regular library users by including an announcement in the area's local parents' newspaper.

Storytimes for Preschoolers

As in the case of programs for adults, storytimes for preschoolers are offered both inside and outside of the library. For decades librarians have conducted daytime preschool storytimes in libraries, usually in mid-morning or in early afternoon. Today more libraries are conducting evening and Saturday storytimes in order to reach the children of working parents. For some libraries, publicity for the evening and weekend storytimes through the preschools, child care centers, and agencies that work with disabled preschoolers has proven to be an effective way of informing working parents.

Aware that many working parents are still unable to bring children to storytimes, librarians bring storytimes to children at preschools and child care centers. In this way, children experience a storytime, and teachers and child care personnel learn more about librarians, books, storytime techniques, and other types of library service. In some cases librarians will ask teachers and child care personnel if their children will be involved with a special project or event and will plan the storytime accordingly. By having an immediate relationship to the project or event, the storytime will not only be more meaningful to the children but, more importantly, it will demonstrate to the adults how storytimes can tie into their curricula.

Librarians often bring bookmarks for children at the preschools and centers. When children bring these home, their parents know that the librarian was at the center or preschool. Promotional information on the bookmarks about upcoming library programs along with the library's location and hours has been helpful in bringing parents and preschoolers into the library.

An important complement to preschool storytimes is the encouragement of adults to repeat storytime books and activities in the home, preschool or child care center. Therefore, adults should be given handouts which contain storytime contents whether or not they have attended the storytime with their children.

Storytime kits prepared by librarians and loaned to teachers and caregivers of preschoolers are an effective means of promoting storytimes at preschools and centers. The kits often include some or all of the following: books, flannel board story characters and stories, simple finger and hand puppets that are used while reciting a poem or nursery rhyme, story-related activity ideas, lists and directions of finger plays, musical cassettes, and booklists. The contents of the circulating story-time kits are materials that have been used by librarians with preschoolers. Some libraries prepare kits focused on themes such as weather, pets, transportation, etc. (A listing of appropriate theme topics can be found in the Schema in Chapter 5.) Such kits provide teachers and caregivers with ready-made model storytimes that they can share with their preschoolers.

Planning, Implementing, and Evaluating Programs: A Checklist

The following checklist may be used to help librarians when they are considering initiating or continuing a library program. It is general and can be adapted to particular library settings.

Where to Begin?

1. Have you defined the goal of children's services and the role(s) the library will play?
2. Have you conducted an evaluation or self-study of:
   - The population?
   - The collection?
   - Staffing and scheduling?
   - Existing programs for children?
   - Existing programs for adults?
   - Existing program priorities?

Planning

1. Have you collected information about the community?
   - What other community agencies exist that offer educational services to preschoolers and their parents, teachers, and caregivers?
   - Is there need for these programs?
2. Have you collected information about the library and the children's department or area?

- – Are there adequate facilities for programs?
- – Is there an adequate collection to support programs?
- – Is there adequate knowledgeable staff for programs?
- – Is there an adequate budget allocation for programs?

3. Have you documented the need for programs?
4. What are the goals of the programs? (A goal is long-range and represents a vision of excellence in library service.)
5. What are the objectives of the programs? (Objectives are specific, time limited, and measurable or verifiable.)

Implementation

1. Have you identified possible programs to help fulfill the goals and objectives?
2. Have you selected programs best suited to the library's circumstances and resources, taking into account the scopes of the programs and institutional factors?
3. Have you developed the programs, identifying such factors as:
   - – The audience, including those with disabilities?
   - – The time of day and date, or dates if it is to be a series?
   - – The type of publicity to be used?
   - – The type of registration, if any, to be used?
   - – The contents of the programs?
   - – Materials needed for programs and for adults such as reading lists or copies of a listing of activities included?
   - – Space and equipment needed?
   - – Staff needed to conduct programs while still providing adequate coverage of the children's area; and staff needed for support services, such as clerical help or artwork?
   - – Funds required for the cost for materials, collection development, additional staff, etc.?

4. Have you enlisted the support of the administration and the cooperation of departments and staff throughout the library?

5. Have you established an implementation schedule?

6. Has staff been assigned responsibilities to accomplish the implementation?

7. Is the implementation being adequately managed?
   - Are staff members being responsible for accomplishing tasks on time?
   - Are output measures being collected?

Evaluation

1. Have you conducted a review of the programs?
   - Were costs as expected?
   - Was the estimate of staff's time accurate? If not, why not?
   - How did staff involvement in the programs affect other types of library service and operations?
   - Were program announcements well-timed and adequate? Were they overdone?

2. Have you identified the extent to which each objective was met?

3. Have you identified factors that have contributed to the success or failure of accomplishing objectives?

4. Have you summarized this information, either formally or informally?

8

A Selection of Annotated References

Child Development Resources

Ames, Louise Bates and Frances L. Ilg. *Your Three-Year-Old: Friend or Enemy*. New York: Delacorte, 1976. *Your Four-Year-Old: Wild and Wonderful*. New York: Delacorte, 1976.
Louise Ames and the late Frances Ilg worked with Arnold Gesell, the well-known psychologist, "baby doctor" of the 1940s, physician, and researcher. Much of the material in these books can also be found in Gesell, Ilg, and Ames's *Infant and Child in the Culture of Today: The Guidance of Development in Home and Nursery School*, rev. ed. (New York: Harper & Row, 1974).

Aries, Philippe. *Centuries of Childhood: A Social History of Family Life*. Translated by Robert Baldick. New York: Knopf, 1962.
The author, who studied the development of the concept of childhood, contends that the concept did not exist until the seventeenth century. This classic has served as a basis for many historical studies of childhood.

Brearley, M. and E. Hitchfield. *A Guide to Reading Piaget*. New York: Schocken, 1966.
Piaget's concepts are presented in an easy-to-understand style by topics such as moral development, number, and measurement. The sample quotations from Piaget's

writings incorporated throughout the book convey his
eloquent though often difficult style.

Chukovsky, Kornei. *From Two to Five.* Berkeley: University of
California Press, 1963.
The classic work by the well-known Russian author and
children's poet describes the verbal creativity of preschoolers and captures the excitement they experience as
they learn to use language.

de Villiers, Peter A. and Jill G. *Early Language.* Cambridge,
Mass.: Harvard University Press, 1979.
The authors provide a lucid, balanced, and entertaining
account of this complex, fascinating subject.

Erikson, Erik. *Childhood and Society.* 2nd rev. ed. New York:
Norton, 1963.
The author, a psychoanalyst, teacher, and writer,
expounds his theory of the relationship between early
child-rearing practices and the growth of personality
and character. A classic.

Hunt, J. McVicker. *Intelligence and Experience.* New York:
Ronald, 1961.
This scholarly treatment of the heredity-environment
controversy by a respected researcher played a leading
role in spreading the ideas of Piaget in this country. This
classic is worth rereading.

Leach, Penelope. *Your Baby and Child from Birth to Age Five.* New
York: Knopf, 1977.
This comprehensive child care book for parents, written
by a noted English psychologist and child development
expert, is one of the best.

Piaget, Jean and Barbel Inhelder. *The Psychology of the Child.*
New York: Basic Books, 1969.
An excellent summary of Piaget's theories of cognitive
development by the master himself. *Play, Dreams, and
Imitation* (New York: Norton, 1951) which describes the

"preoperational" period of development may be of
interest to those who want additional information about
the preschool period.

Early Childhood Education Resources

Butler, Dorothy. *Cushla and Her Books*. Boston: Horn Book, 1980.
When the author learned that her four-month-old
granddaughter had multiple handicaps, she began
reading to her. This book is an account of their experiences and a testimonial to the powerful influence that
books had on Cushla.

Eliason, Claudia F. and Loa Thomson Jenkins. *A Practical Guide
to Early Childhood Curriculum*. 3rd ed. Columbus, Ohio:
Merrill, 1986.
This textbook which blends the theory and application
of early childhood education contains a curriculum for
children from three to six years of age based on appropriate developmental abilities. It is useful for librarians
who work with preschools or who are looking for story
program topics.

Elkind, David. *The Hurried Child: Growing up Too Fast, Too Soon*.
Reading, Mass.: Addison-Wesley, 1981.
The author points out factors in contemporary life that
cause children to feel hurried and under stress. He advocates that children be allowed to experience childhood, and makes a case for the role of play.

Montessori, Maria. *The Discovery of the Child*. Translated by M.J.
Costelloe. Notre Dame, Ind.: Fides, 1967.
One of the many books written by Montessori. This provides a comprehensive overview and serves as a useful
introduction.

Spodek, Bernard, Olivia N. Saracho, and Richard C. Lee.
Mainstreaming Young Children. Belmont, Cal.: Wadsworth,,
1984.

Even though this book is written for early childhood
teachers who work with disabled children in their
classes, librarians will find useful material about specific
types of disabilities and educational needs of handicapped preschoolers.

Organizations

Association for Childhood Education International
11141 Georgia Avenue
Wheaton, MD 20902
ACEI works for the education of children from birth to
fourteen years of age. Publications include *Childhood
Education* and bulletins on current topics in education.

National Association for the Education of Young Children
1834 Connecticut Avenue, NW
Washington, DC 20009
NAEYC focuses on educational services and resources
for children from birth to eight years of age. Publications
include *Young Children*, books, and pamphlets on topics
concerned with young children.

Literary and Literacy Development Resources

Bissex, Glenda L. *GNYS AT WRK: A Child Learns to Write and
Read.* Cambridge, Mass.: Harvard University Press, 1980.
This is an account of how one child learns to read and
write beginning at age five. The book's title comes from
a sign the child posted on his door: "DO NAT DSTRB
GNYS AT WRK." Librarians who want to know more
about the development of writing should read this.

Butler, Dorothy. *Babies Need Books.* New York: Atheneum, 1980.
The author, a teacher, parent, grandmother, and children's bookseller in New Zealand, passionately believes
that books should play a crucial role in children's lives
and offers ways in which they can be used with young
children.

Butler, Dorothy and Marie Clay. *Reading Begins at Home: Preparing Children for Reading Before They Go to School.* Exeter, N.H.: Heinemann, 1982.

The New Zealand authors direct this slim book at parents of preschoolers and offer valuable suggestions. Clay, who used the term "emergent literacy" in her 1966 doctoral dissertation, has written extensively on the relationship between writing and reading in early literacy development.

Clark, Margaret M. *Young Fluent Readers: What Can They Teach Us?* Exeter, N.H.: Heinemann, 1976.

The author, a Scottish psychologist, undertook a study to determine the extent to which certain characteristics played a role in helping children learn to read at an early age. "The important role played by the local library in catering for and in stimulating the interests of these children is certainly one striking feature of the study." (p. 103)

Dalgliesh, Alice. *First Experiences with Literature.* New York: Scribner, 1932.

A well-known writer of children's books, reviewer, and educator, examines the characteristics of young children and literature for them in this classic. Introduction by Patty Smith Hill. Well worth a rereading.

Freeman, G. LaVerne and Ruth S. Freeman. *The Child and His Picture Book: A Discussion of the Preferences of the Nursery Child.* Chicago: Northwestern University Press, 1933.

This is the best one of the handful of studies on picture book preferences conducted during the thirties. Using 120 picture books by Elsa Beskow, Leslie Brooke, Caldecott, Walter Crane, Wanda Ga'g, Bertha and Elmer Hader, Mary Steichen Martin, Jessie Willcox Smith, Blanche F. Wright and others, the examiner asked 60 three-, four-, and five-year-olds which ones out of pairs of pictures they liked better. Results indicated that

preschoolers preferred realistic pictures, but not photographs, with an intensity of color and with figures that
were strongly outlined and given a simplified treatment;
children also favored illustrations with simple and
familiar objects and with children playing together or
engaged in manipulative activity each with an obvious
"story." A historical curiosity.

Goelmann, Hillel, Antoinette Oberg, and Frank Smith, eds.
Awakening to Literacy. Portsmouth, N.H.: Heinemann, 1984.
Fourteen papers written by advocates of the early literacy movement, such as Jerome Bruner, Yetta Goodman,
and Frank Smith, constitute a review of the research on
literacy before schooling.

Holdaway, Don. *The Foundations of Literacy*. Exeter, N.H.:
Heinemann, 1979.
The ideas of this noted teacher and lecturer first gained
prominence in New Zealand and Australia. Holdaway
takes the sharing of stories as the cornerstone of his
multifunctional literacy program. Even though its
intended audience is teachers, the book is useful to
librarians who are interested in literacy theories and
practices. Chapter 3, which discusses literacy learning
before formal schooling is excellent.

Mitchell, Lucy Sprague. *Here and Now Story Book: Two- through
Seven-Year-Olds*. New York: Dutton, 1921. Rev. and
enlarged ed., 1948.
A pioneer book made up of a collection of stories which
"was written to give young children pleasure and
stimulus toward further observation and learning
through hearing and thinking about those things which
chiefly interest them in their own world." The stories
are dated and of historical interest, but the 42-page
essay, "What Language Means to Young Children—To
Parents, Teachers, and Writers," is worth careful
reading. Mitchell's argument that anthropomorphism,

fairy tales, and stories of magic are inappropriate for young children is persuasive.

Morrow, Lesley Mandel. *Literacy Development in the Early Years: Helping Children Read and Write.* Englewood Cliffs, N.J.: Prentice-Hall, 1989.
Morrow provides research findings, descriptions, and opinions about early literacy and suggests ways that schools and homes can promote early literacy.

Schickedanz, Judith A. *More Than the ABCs: The Early Stages of Reading and Writing.* Washington, D.C.: National Association for the Education of Young Children, 1986.
This highly readable handbook recommends the kinds of picture books and writing materials preschoolers should have and suggests ways of creating environments that foster their use.

Taylor, Denny. *Family Literacy: Young Children Learning to Read and Write.* Exeter, N.H.: Heinemann, 1983.
In research focusing on children that are early readers, the author finds evidence about how the family naturally promotes the development of literacy in children to the point that it "is a part of the very fabric of family life."

Teale, William H., and Elizabeth Sulzby, eds. *Emergent Literacy: Writing and Reading.* Norwood, N.J.: Ablex, 1986.
This collection of chapters examines the beginnings of literacy from various perspectives. Of special interest are those by the editors, who provide a summary of the history of emergent literacy; Denny Taylor, who looks at what happens during family storybook reading; and Catherine E. Snow and Anat Ninio, who focus upon the effects on language acquisition of parent-child interactions during picture story book reading.

Weekes, Blanche E. *Literature and the Child.* New York: Silver, Burdett, 1935.

Chapter VI, "The Child's First Literature," debates the education question of the 1930s: Should young children be read folk and modern fairy tales? Written by a professor of elementary education.

Wells, Gordon. *The Meaning Makers: Children Learning Language and Using Language to Learn.* Portsmouth, N.H.: Heinemann, 1986.
Using results from fifteen years of longitudinal research in Great Britain, the author reports on the importance of books and reading aloud during early childhood for later educational gains. Wells shows that the most important predictor of reading comprehension at age seven was the frequency of listening to stories in earlier years. Chapter 10, "The Sense of Story," is especially relevant for librarians.

White, Dorothy. *Books before Five.* Portsmouth, N.H.: Heinemann, 1954, 1984.
White, a librarian, records how she and her daughter Carol shared books during the early childhood years. The new edition of this delightful classic has a foreword by Marie Clay.

Library Service and Programs Resources

American Library Association. Association for Library Service to Children. Preschool Services and Parent Education Committee. *First Steps to Literacy: Library Programs for Parents, Teachers, and Caregivers.* Chicago: American Library Association, 1990.
Guidelines and specifics are provided about seven different library programs for adults who do or will care for young children—high schoolers, expectant parents, parents and caregivers, etc.

American Library Association. Association for Library Service to Children. Program Support Publications Committee. *Programming for Children with Special Needs.* Chicago:

American Library Association, 1981. *Programming for Three-to Five-Year-Olds.* Chicago: American Library Association, 1983. *Programming to Introduce Adults to Children's Literature.* Chicago: American Library Association, 1981.

These four- to five-page publications cover the major points about their respective topics.

Eldridge, Leslie, ed. *R Is for Reading: Library Service to Blind and Physically Handicapped Children.* Washington, D.C.: Library of Congress, National Library Service for the Blind and Physically Handicapped, 1985.

This government document, available from the Reference Section of NLS, Library of Congress, Washington D.C. 20542, is a collection of interviews with blind and physically disabled children, their mothers, teachers, reading specialists, and librarians concerning materials for reading. The book describes the difficulties disabled children face in using braille and large print books, and cassettes. The importance of library service to disabled preschoolers is stressed.

MacDonald, Margaret Read. *Booksharing: 101 Programs to Use with Preschoolers.* Hamden, Conn.: Library Professional Publications, 1988.

A comprehensive resource providing titles of books, poems, recordings, etc. for library storytimes according to theme for preschoolers.

Myers, Garry Cleveland and Clarence W. Sumner. *Books and Babies.* Chicago: McClurg, 1938.

The authors describe their philosophy of the library's role in serving parents of young children and the literature to support the effort. Based on Myers's research as a psychologist and Sumner's work as a librarian who founded a Mothers' Room in a public library in the twenties. Sumner's *The Birthright of Babyhood* (New York: Thomas Nelson, 1936) contains much of the same

information. Both are delightful reading and worth the
time required to locate them.

Start Early for an Early Start. Edited by Ferne Johnson. Chicago:
American Library Association, 1976.
A collection of short articles on characteristics of young
children, and books, materials, and library service for
them.

Organizations

Association for Library Service to Children
50 E. Huron Street
Chicago, IL 60611
ALSC, a division of the American Library Association, is
the major professional library association for those
involved with public library service for children from
birth to adolescence. Publications include *Journal of
Youth Services in Libraries*, books, and pamphlets on
topics concerning children and library service.

Index